LEAVING GLORY FOR GREATNESS

The True Story of
All-American Athlete
Turned Activist,
LaMarr Thomas

MICHIGAN STATE

36

ECKHARTZ
PRESS

Lou Macaluso

ISBN: 979-8-9861972-5-8

Dedicated to the memory of Clarence and Frances Thomas,
loving parents of LaMarr, Tina and Everett

TO AN EX-FOOTBALL STAR
– TO LAMARR THOMAS

They have
No use for him
Now.
    He refuses
To bring them
Glory in the same way.

On their T.V.
They can't point
To him and
Add to themselves.

He was their man,
Their favorite American
Boy,
    Until he started
Looking inside
At someone else.
    They
Couldn't understand
How he could blow all
That Pro money
Running up and down the field
With the pigskin.   Couldn't
Understand; He must be crazy!

But he knew
Where he was coming
From.

Standing alone,

Leaning up against that tree
By that lake in Minnesota
He knew.

And when he went
Running off that evening
to watch the sun
Sinking to the lake's bottom,

I knew
He wouldn't ever be turned
On by that pigskin
Again.

– Dr. Richard W. Thomas

ACKNOWLEDGEMENTS

Christine LaVette Thomas and Tina Thomas, LaMarr's wife and sister, respectively, made this book possible. They shared their memories and their hearts.

Thanks to Dr. Robert L. Green, LaMarr's mentor and friend who helped shape his character as a scholar and human rights activist.

Thanks to LaMarr's lifelong friends since his boyhood: HK (Harry) Hall, Victor Jackson, Linnetta Taylor, Harry Oryhon, and Cyrus Joyner; high school friends and teammates: Ray Jakubiak, Carl Barnhill, Jane Martin, and Lou Boudreau. Michigan State University friends: Richard and June Thomas, Barry Amis, and Claire McClinton; MSU football teammates: Charles Bailey, Earl Anderson, and William Triplett; Thornton Alumni Legacy Fund (TALF) members: Eric Fox, Lorna Propes, Carl Durnavich, and Dale Mize.

A special thanks to Tom Dreesen and Dan Ustian.

All the following people added to the writing of this book: Lawrence (Pudgy) Powell, Clarence Hayes, Denard Eaves, Jack Browers, Mike Talaga, Tim Lau, Dean Mitchell, Kamala Buckner, Roger Wexelberg, Dorinda Urbauer, Mark Gary, Beth Kendall, Whitney Miller--Michigan State University Archives & Historical Collections, Tony Dudek, Senior Account Executive—Tribune Content Agency, Drew Altizer—Drew Altizer Photography, The AP Images Sales Team, Paulette Martis, Kara Fisher, and Matt Larson—MSU Athletic Communications, Claudia Vazquez and Ben Godwin— Catapult Sports Company, Melanie Krakauer, Director of Communications—Illinois Policy Institute, Wesley Herold—State News, Tom Hartmann—Blink of an Eye Productions, Bruce Firchau—Illinois Basketball Coaches' Association.

Thanks to Eckhartz Press and its founders, Rick Kaempfer and David Stern.

PROLOGUE

Friday, May 8, 2015

LaMarr and I stood side-by-side before separate urinals in the men's room at Idlewild Country Club, just south of Chicago.

I wish the setting for our first encounter was more dignified. NBA/ABA star Jim Ard had met LaMarr on a basketball court in Harvey, Illinois. Comedian/actor/writer Tom Dreesen met LaMarr on a golf course during a charity event LaMarr helped organize for underprivileged teens.

Nevertheless, LaMarr and I stood next to each other and complied with a longstanding unwritten rule among males when using urinals: NO CONVERSATION. It's a respected statute for one good reason: There's nothing to say. Even innocent comments such as, "How's it going?" or "Nice to see you here," sound awkward.

We continued our pantomime at the wash basins when a club member entered the restroom. His sunburned face, short-sleeved Polo shirt, and Titleist visor revealed that he was a golfer.

"Hey, I feel a little underdressed in here next to you guys in suits and ties. What's the occasion in the banquet room?" he asked.

"We and some others are being inducted into the Thornton High School Hall of Fame," I said.

"I knew a lot of old-timers like us who graduated from there. Any names I'd know?"

I looked at LaMarr's lavaliere name tag. It was turned the wrong way so I reached over and twisted it, revealing his identity in bold, black caps: LAMARR THOMAS.

The sunburned country club golfer turned into a starstruck little boy.

"Wow, you're him? I mean, I'm not even from this area. I went to school in southern Illinois, and I remember that name. Hell, everyone in the Midwest remembers that name. Let's see,

you were an all-state football and basketball player, a high school All-American, the leading rusher at Michigan State bound for the NFL, and . . ."

His face grew pale.

"And . . . what . . . what happened?"

PART 1:

LIVING IN A BUBBLE

CHAPTER 1

Summer, 1960

LaMarr leaned forward and looked for the sign from the catcher, his younger brother, Everett. It almost seemed unfair that eleven-year-old LaMarr Thomas, with such a tall, muscular body, should be permitted to play Little League baseball. Everett, smaller and two years LaMarr's junior, flashed one finger between his legs.

Fastball.

LaMarr had a big decision. Does he adhere to Everett's request before the game, or does he go with his heart? He made his decision, wound up, and delivered the pitch. The ball seemed to disappear when it left his fingertips, and when it hit the catcher's mitt, a loud, dull thud could be heard in the stands.

Before the umpire could call it a ball or a strike, an angry ballplayer rushed from home plate and charged the mound. It was not the batter; rather, it was brother Everett. Leaving his glove and mask behind, Everett's fists tightened as he sprinted toward the pitcher's mound.

LaMarr stepped forward and waited for the attack. With athletic precision, he bent at the waist just as Everett attempted a punch. Everett's momentum carried him over LaMarr's back, and he landed on the mound.

Coach McNeal stood between them and addressed Everett, "What's wrong with you, son?"

"He throws too hard. I told him not to throw so hard. Look at my hand," he said, showing his reddened palm to the coach.

"Get a pad or a thicker glove. He's supposed to throw hard, and you're the catcher. You're supposed to—"

"It doesn't matter. I quit!"

Everett walked toward the dugout.

The coach tried to follow, but LaMarr touched his arm and said, "Hold on, Coach. Let me handle this."

LaMarr followed Everett off the field and said, "Stop."

Everett halted but didn't turn to face his brother. Even as a boy, LaMarr had a quiet, controlled way of talking that could bring a listener to tears. Everett wouldn't let his big brother see him cry.

"I'm not going to apologize. You're a really good ballplayer, Everett. I'd never ask you to be anything less. You always have to do what's best for the team, not just what's best for you."

LaMarr walked back to the mound. He would live by these words for the rest of his life, but it became harder and harder as he matured.

He leaned forward and waited for a sign from a new catcher.

CHAPTER 2

March 1957

A few houses, cornfields, and no streetlights.

That's what six-year-old Tina and her two older brothers, Everett and LaMarr, saw when they stood on the front lawn of their new home in Markham, just ten miles south of the Chicago city limits.

Clarence Thomas moved his family there from their home at 64th and Drexel (Woodlawn) on the advice of a Chicago policeman/friend who had also purchased a house in Markham. At that time, Woodlawn had been a safe, respectable southside Chicago neighborhood, but Clarence and his wife, Frances, wanted better schools and opportunities for their kids. Markham and the other south suburbs within Thornton Township promised those things.

Clarence worked for one of the many Schlitz Brewery distributors in the Chicago area. Milwaukee, just across the Wisconsin-Illinois border, housed the main brewery, but Chicago, with its restaurants, liquor stores, and neighborhood taverns, provided the major market. From 1947 and throughout the 1950s and 60s, Schlitz held first place as the largest American brewery. Consequently, its employees, including Clarence, enjoyed steady employment, decent wages, and fringe benefits.

His reputation as a gifted baseball player followed him from Memphis to Chicago. He commanded his family with a big heart and a heavy hand and encouraged his children to excel in both sports and academics.

Chicago-born Frances shared her husband's charitable heart. Known as a talented chef, she often cooked for others as well as her own family. "LaMarr adored his momma," Tina would say, and Frances was "the glue that held the family together."

Markham was a culture shock for the Thomas children. Its rural roots and dirt roads clashed with the apartment buildings, the busy 63rd Street business sector, and the Woodlawn Movie Theater just around the corner from their former dwelling. Heavily and diversely populated Harvey on the north and predominately white-populated Hazel Crest on the south bordered the small Markham community where they now lived.

LaMarr, Everett, and Tina would attend Warren Palm Elementary School in Hazel Crest. Walking through all-white Hazel Crest, they experienced no racial conflicts on their way to and from school. African/American children made up about thirty percent of the Warren Palm student body. "Living in Markham was like living in a bubble. We didn't go through a lot of things other black people went through," Tina said years later.

LaMarr was the biggest kid in his third-grade class. His shy nature clashed with his intimidating presence, and everyone in class, including his teacher, Miss Elswick, admired him. One chubby little Greek boy, Harry Oryhon, quarreled with the new big kid in the boys' room after recess. LaMarr called him something such as a "little runt," and Harry returned with a word he had heard in his neighborhood when referring to black people.

"You're a nigger!" he said.

LaMarr chased him down the hall.

Harry dodged between students returning to class and ducked into the cloak room in the back of their classroom. He felt safe hiding behind a long coat hanging on a hook. He must have forgotten that the bottoms of his corduroy pants and his Buster Brown shoes stuck out beneath the garment, and he felt a solid punch in his stomach that doubled him over in pain. Both boys were suspended, but two positive outcomes emerged. Harry learned the negative connotation and the emotionally charged impact of the "n" word, and a lifelong friendship developed between him and LaMarr.

More black families moved to Markham from Chicago that summer. The Halls and the Jacksons had migrated there from Altgeld Gardens, a far southside neighborhood made famous years later when a young community organizer, Barack Obama, worked with the residents for better living conditions. Harry, who would later legally change his first name to HK, Hall and Victor Jackson befriended LaMarr, a year younger than them.

"LaMarr was a little stronger than all of us. He didn't have an older brother, so he looked at me as a guy he could rely on," HK remembered.

The boys invented games to fill the summer months. They cleared an abandoned cornfield and carved out a baseball diamond. The "World Series" between the eastside and westside of Markham took place every summer. Fathers, including Clarence, recognized the boys' baseball interest and organized a Little League chapter. LaMarr and HK were teammates.

"We used to go rabbit hunting," Victor recalled. "We were in this cornfield, and we'd hunt with sticks and rocks, not guns. The owner of the land would come out shooting a shotgun, and we'd all run. LaMarr, because of his size and look, looked like he could be a [young] gangster."

Victor and HK introduced LaMarr to a new game, basketball.

Most of the boys LaMarr's age were too short to enjoy shooting at the basket, but LaMarr was taller and more athletic. "Harry [HK] and I had outstanding coaches all the way through grade school. They trained us on the basics. I mean we were kicking the ball, bouncing it off our heads, and these coaches just took us to the side and gifted us. They saw something [in us] that we didn't see . . . and we ended up liking it. It was amazing," Victor said.

While most kids mourned the end of summer, LaMarr's love for learning and his teachers intensified his enthusiasm for the start of the school year. Mr. Sidmore, the gym teacher, instituted basketball into the fourth-grade physical education curriculum and recognized LaMarr's advanced skills.

LaMarr unveiled another hidden talent - singing. At an all-school talent contest, LaMarr impersonated Elvis. His melodic voice mesmerized the kids and gave him the confidence to join the choir at Christ Temple Church where his family worshipped.

When not playing sports, singing, or listening in class, LaMarr often sat at the kitchen table and read science-fiction books, or history books, or the Bible. His new life in Markham seemed perfect, however, a harsh reality would hit him one Saturday afternoon.

Saturdays meant visiting Grandma in Bronzeville, a famous southside Chicago neighborhood. Bronzeville was well-known for its rich Black American culture. Nat King Cole, Richard Wright, Sam Cooke, Quincy Jones, and many more Black artists once lived in Bronzeville. In the late 50s and early 60s, Bronzeville became legendary for a less celebrated trait—gang violence.

LaMarr, Everett, and a cousin played basketball at an outdoor public court near their grandmother's home. LaMarr wanted to share and teach the skills he had learned from HK, Victor, and

Coach Sidmore. After a missed shot, the ball rolled off the court and into the hands of a tall teenager.

"Thanks for finding my basketball," he said.

"It's our ball," LaMarr said, stepping towards him. "Could you please throw it back?"

That ended the conversation. Several more teens exited a parked car, and they all attacked LaMarr and stole his ball. His physical injuries were minor, but the incident left a traumatic emotional scar.

He barely spoke until they returned home to Markham.

"No more Chicago," he said and slammed the car door shut.

CHAPTER 3

C-r-r-a-a-ck— the sound of the breaking brittle tiles on Ferguson's Tavern's roof a couple hundred feet from the Warren Palm playground. Thirteen-year-old LaMarr was the only kid in either the seventh or eighth grade who could hit the cushy sixteen-inch softball from home plate to that leaky, rotting rooftop, but instead of rounding the bases, he and the rest of the kids would rush inside the school building in fear that the owner, Al Ferguson, would come out and raise hell.

Ferguson's Tavern, located between Warren Palm Elementary School and St. Anne's Catholic Church, had been erected long before the city council adopted an ordinance: "No village retail liquor dealer's license of any kind shall be issued under any of the following conditions: For use on premises adjacent to churches, schools, and hospitals." A court ruling allowed the tavern to keep its liquor license under an existing "grandfather clause." The city avenged the court ruling by refusing to issue a building permit for any major improvements or repairs, so all damages remained permanent. Consequently, the Fergusons did not appreciate LaMarr's destructive home run power.

By the end of September, Hazel Crest and Markham kids put away their baseballs, softballs, bats, and gloves and tossed footballs around. No formal football programs existed for kids,

---

so they improvised touch and tackle games on playgrounds, plowed cornfields, and in the streets. "No one could touch LaMarr," Lawrence (Pudgy) Powell, a former Markham neighborhood child, said. "After watching us play touch football in the street, my father said to me, 'That kid [LaMarr] is gonna' be something,' and he was right."

Basketball became the most popular sport at Warren Palm. They played year-round, indoors, outdoors, and in all kinds of weather. Winter heralded the opening of the official basketball season, and Coach Sidmore assembled the most formidable grade school teams in the Chicago south suburban area. He had a big heart and accepted every boy who tried out. LaMarr started either at center or forward every game.

"Stay on the big kid" commanded opposing coaches to their player or players assigned to guard LaMarr. It didn't matter. LaMarr could score and steal the ball seemingly at will, but always remained "a team player," recalled a former teammate,

LaMarr, center, holding the trophy. Coach Sidmore, back row, far left. Harry Oryhon, first row, far right.
Photo courtesy of Cyrus Joyner

"sometimes to a fault. [LaMarr] wide open under the basket, might pass to Ken (Parker) or Terry (Kinas), also open, just so they had a chance to score too."

"No one could beat us," said Harry Oryhon.

LaMarr's popularity caused positive and negative consequences. Girls gravitated to him. Tina recalled, "He liked girls, but he was shy. Everett and I were the outgoing ones. We taught him to dance. Then, this girl moved out here and she kind of got him out of being shy. Something about her drew him out." At the same time, his popularity proved troublesome for his siblings who also attended Warren Palm. Tina and Everett inherited the Thomas gene for athleticism, but not to the extent as LaMarr. "Why can't you be more like your big brother?" became a common criticism from coaches and teachers throughout grade school and high school. Everett felt the sting of those comments throughout his life.

As his eighth-grade year ended, LaMarr became more intense. His temper often flared. During a verbal dispute with his mother, Frances told him, "You're going to be like your father (known for an explosive temper)."

"No, I'm not," LaMarr answered, but he couldn't be sure.

Things got worse for LaMarr and Everett. In their old neighborhood, Woodlawn, abandoned buildings were "attractive nuisances" for kids. In Markham, the opposite was true.

"We used to play in the new homes as they were being built," HK said.

LaMarr, Everett, and other neighborhood boys accidentally started a fire in a house construction project. Police arrived and apprehended the youths. Clarence was called to take custody of his sons at the Markham Police Station.

"He beat the brains out of them," Tina remembered.

She also recalled an epiphany LaMarr experienced that

summer at a camp. "I don't remember where he went, but when he came back, he promised he was going to be a different person. He was less explosive. He was a gentle giant. He didn't holler and scream anymore, but he wasn't a pushover either. He could look you right in the eye and make you cry. He didn't want to be volatile like his father, so he learned to channel that rage."

Specifically, he channeled his rage through sports. He competed with a near-unconscious fervor that intimidated opponents. At the same time, he calmed his spirit by singing and supporting his teammates with words of encouragement such as, "Nice shot" or "Good effort." By the end of summer, 1962, LaMarr felt more comfortable with himself. When he stepped onto the bus for his first day at high school, he felt ready, but he had a major surprise coming.

CHAPTER 4

September 4, 1962, 7:30 a.m.

The school bus turned off 150th Street onto Broadway Avenue in Harvey, Illinois. With a dozen other buses, it parked along the curb on the west side of the school building. Buses lined Main Street on the east side of the structure also. The second fleet would arrive in minutes. LaMarr looked out the window of his filled-to-capacity bus at the three-story, block-long school building.

Thornton Township High School (TTHS) educated the Chicago south suburban teen population from Riverdale to Kankakee (fifty miles apart) when it opened in 1899. Despite the school district boundaries tightening over the decades, the enrollment continued to grow until the district built Thornridge High School in 1960, which reduced Thornton's enrollment by half. Nevertheless, the building of new schools couldn't keep up with the waves of baby boomers reaching high school age and by 1962, Thornton Township High School enrolled nearly 3,000 students which would grow to almost 5,000 by 1966.

The high enrollment produced a tremendous pool of athletic talent and teams and made competition fierce. A better-than-average athlete might not have a chance to play or even be on the roster of a TTHS team.

A more important reason TTHS created great athletes and teams was its location, Harvey, Illinois. Turlington W. Harvey founded the city in 1891 and claimed it was a "Gateway to the South Suburbs." He was right. Over the next seventy years, dozens of factories popped up within its six-and-a-half square miles and attracted blue-collar families and residential construction. Prominent department stores, food stores, restaurants, banks, jewelry stores, and two movie theaters lined 154th Street, the main commercial thoroughfare. The Illinois Central Railroad commuter train stopped at the east end of Harvey, so white-collar residents living in more affluent housing on 155th and 150th streets could commute to Chicago's downtown Loop within twenty-five minutes. In the 1960s, the city hosted the development of Dixie Square, a lucrative enclosed shopping mall made famous when the premises were used for the chase scene in the 1978 *Blues Brothers* movie. All this meant tax dollars, some of which went directly to Thornton Township High School.

"We were fortunate to be at Thornton," Victor Jackson remembered. "It was like a college—the facilities: three basketball gyms, swimming pools, underground tunnels to facilities. That was the beauty of Harvey being an industrial town with a large tax base. We thought every high school had that."

The athletic department provided more than facilities, uniforms, and equipment. Most high schools expected the parents of athletes to furnish accessories: proper footwear, practice garments, etc. TTHS supplied top-notch football shoes, basketball sneakers, track spikes, and even clean underwear for practices. "Jimmy, I need a roll" meant that after practice, if you had thrown your soiled sweat socks, jockstrap, and t-shirt into the laundry gurney, Jimmy Heimlich, the equipment custodian, issued you a clean set of tightly rolled garments.

Two weeks before the start of the school year, LaMarr and

about a couple hundred boys tried out for the freshman football team; only sixty would make the final cut. Coaches Dick Bruno and Ted Czech saw the talent in LaMarr, but it was raw talent. Neither Warren Palm nor any of the Illinois public elementary schools had football teams. Several community park districts sponsored junior football leagues for kids under fifteen, but Markham was not among them. Most Catholic elementary schools in the Thornton district did field a team. LaMarr had to learn the football fundamentals: blocking, tackling, taking a hand off, throwing, and carrying the ball. Sandlot football taught him to avoid tacklers, but it didn't teach him the correct stances or the numbering system for the gaps in the offensive line.

The learning curve of football basics and the jammed classrooms and hallways overwhelmed LaMarr. At Warren Palm, he had loved learning and did well in the classroom, but now, his first semester grades suffered. He barely passed his core classes but did well in social studies and gym. His best subject was Glee Club where his singing voice earned him the grade of A.

The football staff decided to harness LaMarr's tremendous size and speed and trained him to be a fullback. By mid-season, he had mastered the basic football skills and developed his unique style of running with the ball. At that time, sports analysts considered Jim Brown the best professional fullback of all time and Gale Sayers the best collegiate running back. LaMarr combined the techniques of both players. Whether or not his offensive linemen blocked for him, LaMarr plowed through the gap in the line. If a linebacker or safety stood in his way, he lowered his shoulder, stunned him with a solid hit, and either pivoted or sidestepped the would-be tackler. He ran the open field until his only obstacle was a goal line.

The freshman team tied for the South Suburban League championship, and LaMarr's name was the only frosh football player in the yearbook: "Fullback LaMarr Thomas aided the future Wildcats to maintain a 6-1 record."

Football season ended and basketball season began. Victor and HK, sophomores from his neighborhood, had earned reputations as top-notch players. Victor described freshman tryouts. "A huge turnout for the basketball team. Huge. Maybe a couple hundred kids or more. They'd call your name with five other guys, five against five. Harry (HK) and I went out. They threw the ball up. The whistle blew. Harry threw me the ball, and I hit a jump shot. The coach said, 'Stop! Are you the two guys who played together at a lower grade championship?' We said, 'Yeah,' and he said, 'Get out. Don't come back until after all this is over.' We didn't have to try out."

LaMarr had a similar experience. Coach Willie Brown had seen him play at Warren Palm and excused LaMarr from trying out, but LaMarr had gained more than just a place on the freshman basketball team; he had acquired a role model. Willie Brown represented the first black adult in his life to have achieved a bachelor's and master's degree and gained fame as a college athlete and scholar. Willie counseled LaMarr throughout high school in sports and academics.

The basketball court felt more like home than the gridiron to LaMarr that first year. Coaches loved that LaMarr could play center, forward, or guard with as good or better ability than any other freshman player. He developed the reputation of an intimidating defensive competitor. When the opposing team had the ball, he seemed to remember the gang members who stole his basketball that Saturday when he was ten years old. "The basketball is mine, and I'm stealing it back!"

He developed team friendships that lasted a lifetime. He and Garland Mays learned to harmonize, and they entertained the team and coaches by singing during bus rides. On the court, he and Richard Halbert created a different type of harmony. Rich had similar incredible basketball skills. His specialties were rebounding and follow-up shooting. Shy like LaMarr, the two bonded, but their shyness evaporated on the court. Each knew precisely when to pass the ball to the other for an open shot or a layup.

Victor and HK, co-captains of the sophomore team, were close by to support LaMarr and the frosh team. Late in the season, Bill Purden, the head varsity coach, brought Vic and HK up to the varsity squad for tournament play. Consequently, the sophomore coach brought tall freshman Bob Landowski to play on his team. The yearbook reported, "Two of his [Landowski's] teammates, LaMarr Thomas and Rich Halbert, were able to make up for the loss as they both played excellent ball. . ."

In June of 1963, LaMarr rode the bus home to Markham after the last day of his first year at Thornton Township High School. He may have recalled how overwhelmed he was by the size of the school, the number of students, and the academic and sports challenges on his first day. On this last day, he felt confident and calm but didn't realize the new tensions he would face at home.

CHAPTER 5

Clarence Thomas had lived most of his young life in Memphis, Tennessee. As an athlete, he recognized exceptional talent. Wayne Wood, Bill Robertson, John Antonelli, Doc Prothro, and many other professional athletes came from Clarence's Memphis neighborhood; however, the "no name" athletes haunted him. These "no names" were athletes who had the talent to become pros but never made it. Alcohol, gambling, poor grades, poor choices, or just being poor sidetracked their sports dreams.

He knew that his fifteen-year-old son LaMarr had the potential to become a professional basketball or football player. He also knew that LaMarr embraced the moral Christian teachings he had learned from his parents and Christ Temple Church. Victor observed, "He wasn't a church goer [in his later teen and adult years], but he had more Christian principles than a preacher." Therefore, Clarence didn't worry about LaMarr making poor choices or engaging in substance abuse. He was concerned about LaMarr's less than stellar grades his freshman year, but he'd make sure LaMarr studied more in the coming years.

Clarence's major concern was the one over which he had the least control. Gifted male athletes with charisma drew the attention of the opposite sex. He had seen many talented athletes lured into fatherhood too early and watched their aspirations implode. As much as he appreciated LaMarr's moral character, he also acknowledged that even the best young men are tempted by sex, and LaMarr had many female admirers to tempt him. His solution was to keep LaMarr close to home. "If you played sports, you got out late, and LaMarr wanted to date. My dad wanted him to come home," Tina recalled. "[Our father] didn't care how good in sports or how popular you were, if you came home late, the door was locked."

Sports and academics kept LaMarr busy. So, providing Clarence enforced his curfew, he didn't have to worry about LaMarr and girls during the school year.

LaMarr celebrated his fifteenth birthday on August 14th of 1963 by reporting for the opening of TTHS football practice. His academic counselor and former freshman basketball coach/role model, Willie Brown, coached the sophomore football team. Willie switched LaMarr's position from fullback to halfback. The change gave LaMarr more running and passing opportunities. He encouraged LaMarr to study more and choose college prep classes. His grades began to improve and he continued to foster his love and talent for singing by joining Thornton's Intermediate Choir.

The TTHS sophomore football team experienced a mediocre 4-4 season. They scored 151 points to their opponents' 101, scoring more than thirty points in each of three games. At the end of the season, a local newspaper, *The South Holland Tribune*, predicted next year's varsity prospects:

> Leading the parade of sophomores will be highly touted halfback LaMarr Thomas who led his mates in scoring for the second consecutive year. Thomas is one of the largest backs to arrive on the scene in some time, tipping the scales at 180 pounds.

Basketball season started a heartbeat away from the end of football season in November. Varsity coach Bill Purden pulled LaMarr's buddy and teammate, Richie Halbert, up to the varsity level for the season. If LaMarr felt any jealousy or animosity about the promotion, he never showed it. He congratulated Richie and cheered him whenever Richie played in a varsity game. Besides, Bob Landowski remained at the sophomore level after moving up from the freshman level the previous year, and Willie Brown's team received an early Christmas gift. Six-foot-eight sophomore Jim Ard transferred from Joliet High School to Thornton in December. Bill Purden decided to season him at the sophomore level instead of bringing him up to the varsity team. Jim would later become a college star at Cincinnati and play professionally for the New York Nets, the Memphis Tams, the Boston Celtics, and the Chicago Bulls. He scored 1909 points and made 1832 rebounds as a pro.

Bob Anderson, sophomore basketball coach, seemed to have a magic touch with his teams. For the third straight year the Thornton soph team took home the conference championship trophy with a 13-1 record. Even in their only loss to Argo High School, 42-44, the local newspaper noted LaMarr's performance.

"LaMarr Thomas, the Kit's leading scorer all season, took honors for the night with 20 points."

LaMarr got an extra boost after his last sophomore game. Coach Purden brought LaMarr and Bob Landowski up to the varsity team for tournament play. The move not only reunited him with Richie Halbert, but also with his Markham buddies, juniors Victor Jackson and Harry (HK) Hall. Victor said, "When you took us undefeated juniors, Harry and me, and combined with LaMarr, no one could stop us."

In the regional tournament, they beat Bremen by 51 points, Sandburg by 24 points, and Eisenhower by 31 points to become regional champs. They won their first game in the sectional tourney but lost the second game by 50-54.

Victor recalled a tradition that LaMarr initiated on the bus rides. "LaMarr and two other guys would sing. They'd sing love songs: The Four Tops, The Temptations. They would harmonize; he was the lead singer. Everything he did was team. He'd bring pieces together and make you comfortable with your role."

After the sectional loss, LaMarr tried to cheer everyone up on the bus with his singing trio. Coach Purden, red-faced, walked back to where they sat and demanded, "Why the hell are you guys singing? We lost!"

Dead silence, and the angry coach returned to his seat.

A veteran varsity team member sitting behind LaMarr leaned forward, said, "Coach Purden just reamed your ass out. Congratulations and welcome to the Thornton Varsity Wildcats," and patted him on the shoulder.

CHAPTER 6

It was sixty degrees and cloudy when the mailman delivered the mail to the Thomas house on June 16th of 1964. Clarence and Frances must have smiled when they read LaMarr's final grades. Contrary to his less-than-mediocre marks the prior year, he ended his sophomore year with a 4.0/5.0 grade point average.

Summer meant more tension between Clarence and LaMarr over dating. LaMarr's August birthday played to Clarence's favor. LaMarr wouldn't be eligible to pass his driver's license test until the end of summer. Consequently, if he wanted to date, he'd have to rely on public transportation or his older friends to drive him. Either way, Clarence enforced his strict curfew restriction year-round.

During that summer, LaMarr seemed to mature and gain status in the neighborhood. He exhibited many of his dad's positive characteristics. "He [Clarence] took care of everybody. Gave to charity. Supported the underdog. Sent money to those who needed it, family or not. [LaMarr] always looked after his brother, sister, and those less fortunate than he. He took after [our] father in that way. Big brother to the whole neighborhood. LaMarr was the protector of everybody," Tina claimed.

During the 60s, Chicago gangs infiltrated the suburbs. The Blackstone Rangers and Eastside Disciples, rooted in the Thomas's previous Woodlawn neighborhood, recruited at Thornton High School and predominately black suburbs such as Markham. LaMarr stood up to gang intimidation, and gang members respected him and other black athletes. Victor explained, "Street gangs were coming up in the neighborhood. Even these little gang members started looking up to us, but some of these guys were good players that waivered off into these gangs."

On the locker room door, Coach Bauman posted the starting lineups for the first varsity season game against Joliet West High School on September 18, 1964. LaMarr's name did not appear on the starting offensive roster. It did exist on the list of starting defensive players. Terry Kinas, an offensive lineman, shook his head and said, "Your name should be on the first-string list, LaMarr."

"Coach knows what's best for the team," LaMarr said, smiled, and entered the locker room.

Another surprise was HK's (Harry Hall's) name on the offensive list as a starting end. HK had never played organized football until this, his senior year. He had gone out for football his freshman year and wanted to play quarterback. The first NFL black quarterback, Martin Briscoe, didn't emerge into pro football until 1968. College and high school football coaches followed that lead and didn't train black players as quarterbacks, clearly a racist decision. HK realized his talents and wouldn't participate in a game that didn't give him the opportunity to prove himself, so he quit.

Three years later, when HK was a senior, Bill Purden, HK's varsity basketball coach, also coached varsity football as an assistant during the 1964 season.

"Purden said, 'Listen, we think we can use you. You're a good athlete, and we think it's going to help you for basketball.' I had good hands and believed him." HK recalled.

This surprised fans and even infuriated some sportswriters. HK was not your average high school basketball player. Some sports journalists hailed him as one of the best high school players in the nation. With the prospect of becoming a great college or pro cager, the decision to lure him into football in his final high school year and to risk injury appeared unwise or downright stupid. The season would tell, and HK would depend on his close friend LaMarr to guide and protect him if he could.

Bauman subbed LaMarr into the backfield during the first half, and LaMarr responded by accumulating sixty-five yards in five carries including a touchdown. The second half, he intercepted a pass on defense and ran back thirty-six yards for another touchdown. Thornton won 18-14.

He had solidified his position as a starting offensive and defensive player.

Heavy rain and a muddy field made running nearly impossible for both teams the following Friday night. Nevertheless, LaMarr carried the ball seven times for 51 yards, averaging 7.3 yards per carry. He and HK each caught a touchdown pass and Thornton beat Eisenhower 20-0.

Thornton had two archrivals, Thornridge and Bloom. When Thornridge opened its doors in 1960, the new boundaries took students living across the street from each other in Riverdale, Dolton, and South Holland and sent them to either TTHS or Thornridge. Within four years, both schools' enrollments had risen to nearly 4,000 again, and the focus of every athletic contest was "Which school was better?" The Thornton-Bloom rivalry had deeper roots. Both schools opened around the turn of the 20th century. Both schools enjoyed a rich industrial tax base within a blue-collar community. The enrollment size and the ethnic demographics were about the same. Like siblings or partners who are too alike to get along, Thornton and Bloom hated each other.

"How about that Harry Hall?" Coach Bauman asked the press after the Thornridge game. The Thornton Wildcats had beaten Thornridge 28-0, but the big story became HK leading the South Suburban League in receptions and LaMarr leading in scoring. Bauman was so engrossed in talking to reporters about LaMarr and HK that the team bus almost left without him.

By the time Thornton and Bloom met on November 7th, Thornton had won all seven of its games, and Bloom had tallied a 6-1 record. Winning meant Thornton would own the championship crown all alone. Losing meant Thornton and Bloom became Co-South Suburban Champions. Four thousand fans crammed into the bleachers and stood inside and outside the stadium fence to watch the game. LaMarr, on a halfback option pass play, hit HK in the endzone on Thornton's first drive. LaMarr rushed for another TD, but it wasn't enough. Bloom won 34-19.

Thornton won their last game against Kankakee and finished as co-champs. The *Harvey Tribune* wrote,

> LaMarr intercepted a pass at the gun near the goal line in which he danced by several defenders, tiptoed the sidelines and hit the end zone flag in only the inimitable LaMarr fashion seen before. LaMarr Thomas perhaps played his finest game of this, or any other season.

The south suburban sportswriters elected LaMarr "Back of the Year" and the only junior on the "All Area Team." Chicagoland coaches also voted him "All-League Back." His season record-breaking stats included nine touchdowns, 459 yards rushing, 11.2 yards per carry, and 95 passing yards. College recruiters from all over the country began contacting Coach Bauman and the Thomas household.

Later, LaMarr would tell reporters that he "ate up" the adulation and "it all went to my head," but no one can testify to that. Everyone recalled LaMarr remaining humble and even reverting to his former shy self. Either way, on November 30, 1964, LaMarr Thomas approached Jimmy Heimlich, equipment custodian, and exchanged his football spikes for a pair of basketball shoes.

Photo courtesy of The Harvey Tribune

CHAPTER 7

Wednesday, December 30, 1964

With four seconds left, Victor Jackson received an inbound pass and drove toward the basket. He saw Richie Halbert open underneath the hoop but decided to take the shot himself. The ball swished through the net at the buzzer, and the Thornton Wildcats secured a third-place trophy at the Centralia, Illinois Holiday Tournament.

"You did it, man!" LaMarr said as he hugged his boyhood buddy and teammate.

"It's about time I did something," Vic later said to the press.

Vic's "golden arm" win, as a sportswriter called it, marked a milestone for the Thornton Wildcats. The previous day they had lost their first game after enjoying an undefeated season.

Before that season, Coach Purden had announced his starting line-up would come from this list: Harry Hall (HK), Victor Jackson, LaMarr Thomas, Rich Halbert, Jim

Victor Jackson
Photo courtesy of
The Harvey Tribune

Ard, Garland Mays, and Larry Seiner—plus, a bench-full of talent. As the season progressed, Purden sized up opponents and chose from that list before and throughout each game. Victor had not performed as well as he had in previous years and didn't play as often as the others; however, after the "golden arm" game, Victor, HK, LaMarr, Richie, and Jim Ard became regulars on the court.

"Knowing each other from the neighborhood, we could rely on each other on the basketball court. We had a winning spirit and attitude," HK recalled.

"Vic looked like a new man on the court," wrote *The Harvey Tribune*, and throughout January, LaMarr, HK, and Victor were the main cogs in what the newspapers called "The Wildcat Machine." The team set several school and state records: most team points scored in a one season, most games with three or more players scoring twenty-plus points and scoring 124 points in a single game. Blowout wins allowed Purden to rotate all fifteen of his players into many of the contests.

But as the season wore down, so did the team. They continued to win but without the same energy and enthusiasm they had previously displayed. With the state playoff series looming ahead, Coach Purden worried. "We are just plain stale," he said.

Leave it to LaMarr. To lift the team's spirits, he and Garland Mays serenaded and led sing-alongs in the locker room and on the bus. The press described what he did on the court:

> A recent spark to Thornton's somewhat sputtering attack has been 6-0 junior guard-forward LaMarr Thomas, who tallied thirteen and nine points in wins over Thornridge and Bloom.

"Don't be too surprised if our effort is not perfect tonight, but we have planned to play these seniors all week," Purden told the press before the last home game of the regular season. He knew he had a talented group of kids, and at the risk of losing another game, he started and played only senior varsity members. His cautionary quote proved meaningless. The all-senior squad scored the second-highest team points for a single game and won 109-60 over Joliet West. Out of love for his teammates, LaMarr thoroughly enjoyed sitting on the bench and cheering HK, Victor, and all the senior players.

At home, tension between LaMarr and his father peaked. Clarence's curfew restriction left little time for socializing after basketball games.

"But Dad, the games and practices go late," LaMarr pleaded.

Clarence didn't budge, and LaMarr took his frustrations out on the court. As an underclassman, the basketball had reminded him of the thugs who had stolen the ball from him when he was ten. Now, the ball represented his freedom as a young adult, and he wanted it back. He became a defensive menace to opposing teams. "How dare you dribble my freedom up the court?" and he'd steal the ball and fastbreak toward the basket.

Preparing for the state playoff series left little time for LaMarr or any of the players to date or just hang out with friends. The Illinois sportswriters had ranked the Thornton Wildcats the number one team in the state, and a few syndicated Chicago writers ranked them first in the nation. Purden worked them long and hard and made them live up to their reputation.

LaMarr and Vic started as guards against their rival, Thornridge, in the regional finals. Purden assigned LaMarr to guard Al Armour, Thornridge's top scorer.

"How many points does Al Armour have?" LaMarr asked Assistant Coach Bob Anderson at halftime.

"Seventeen, and you've only got twelve," he answered.

That hurt LaMarr. People who knew him well were aware

that he was more sensitive than he appeared. It upset him to think that he had let down his coach and team, but he turned his hurt into anger during the second half. Armour didn't score another point and Thornton won 73 to 56.

Next, they became sectional champs defeating Proviso 66-63, and *The Harvey Tribune* credited LaMarr:

"LAMARR THOMAS, a heretofore sticky-fingered defensive star, became a hero with ice water in his veins Friday. Not only did he play fine defense again, but he checked in with more than noteworthy offensive heroics . . . with 19 points."

Only sixteen teams were left in the Illinois High School Association State Basketball Tournament. The Wildcats won their next two games and advanced to the semi-finals in Champaign-Urbana, home of the University of Illinois and the televised tournament. Win or lose, the remaining four teams would have to play two games on Saturday, March 20, 1965: semi-finals in the morning, and consolation and championship games at night.

"It was hard. Two games in one day. Living in a different city, sleeping in a motel. We were just in high school, man, and on an emotional high," Victor recalled.

Thornton lost Saturday morning in the semi-finals and again in the consolation game for third place. They had to settle for the fourth-place state trophy.

The temperature was 23 degrees as the team bus idled outside the main doors of the motel on Sunday morning. Coach Purden counted heads before signaling the driver that all players and coaches had boarded, and they could leave Champaign for Harvey. No one spoke or sang. LaMarr remembered how Coach Purden had chastised him and others for singing after a loss, and they had lost two in a row.

The bus continued up Neil Street, past the Assembly Hall, and into the heart of Champaign-Urbana.

Dead silence.

As the bus approached the ramp onto I-57, the notion hit everyone on the bus at once. The 1965 basketball season was over. Overall, it was a great season. Sure, they had lost a total of three games, two in one day, but they had won so many more. They were the fourth-best team in the state. A parade would greet them in Harvey and lead them to the Thornton gymnasium for a celebration.

It may have been Garland Mays or another member of LaMarr's trio/quartet who hummed the opening of the Temptations most popular song of the year, "Dum, da, da, da, da, da, dum, da, da, da, da, da, dum, da, da, da, da, da—"

"*I've got sunshine on a cloudy day,*" LaMarr sang in a falsetto lead voice.

"*When it's cold outside, I've got the month of May,*" another voice followed.

More joined in, "*I guess you'd say, what could make me feel this way? My girl, my girl, my girl. Talking 'bout my girl . . .*"

LaMarr smiled and closed his eyes. He didn't know it, but before long, he would meet the most important person in his life.

He and others sang all the way home.

CHAPTER 8

Saturday, April 1, 1933

Lou Boudreau didn't know that one day he would be inducted into the Baseball Hall of Fame and immortalized as a player, manager, player/manager, and sportscaster when he strolled down Harvey's primary business district, 154th Street. He only knew that he and his Thornton High School basketball teammates (known as The Flying Clouds) had won the Illinois High School State Basketball Championship the week before. As he and his cronies accepted free ice cream and gifts from Harvey merchants, a stream of admiring children from Warren Palm and Whittier elementary schools followed their heroes throughout the city.

Thirty-two years later, that star-worship of local basketball stars hadn't changed.

"In the cities of Markham and Harvey, when you walked around and played like we did, they treated you like 'Michael Jordans,'" Victor said.

The only basketball heroes in Illinois were the state high school basketball champs. Michael Jordan was only three years old at that time, and the Chicago Bulls wouldn't come into the NBA until a year later.

LaMarr enjoyed the perks of being a local hero which included

---

meeting girls. He found one way to circumvent Clarence's tight curfew enforcement. After participating in Wildcat football and basketball, he traditionally took a well-deserved spring sports season off. That meant no athletic practices after school. A few students who lived adjacent to the school building and whose parents worked nine-to-five jobs hosted get-togethers after the last school bell rang. LaMarr occasionally hung out there.

This year would be different. Victor was a four-year track man. He was part of a mile relay team that was one leg short of becoming a state contender, and he talked LaMarr into joining the team.

"LaMarr ran exceptional times because he was carrying a baton for the team. He would hand it off to me, and I would see this look in his eye. I was the anchor man on this relay. Normally, I'd get the baton, and we were behind, but seeing that look, we went ahead. It was more than athletics. It was heart or something. We broke a record," Victor recalled.

The outdoor track surrounded the football field and Ken Soderquist, a varsity football player, and his girlfriend, junior varsity cheerleader Christine LaVette, watched a track practice from the bleachers. During a break in practice, Ken called LaMarr to the bleachers and introduced him to Chris. "That was the first time I met him," Chris recalled. "I liked him, and he seemed to like me, but nothing came of it at that time."

It's not clear if LaMarr had been dating anyone when he met Chris, but he would not have pursued a relationship with her since she was the girlfriend of a teammate. Nevertheless, neither Chris nor LaMarr ever forgot their first meeting. "It was here at Thornton that I met my fellow classmate and love of my life . . . Chris LaVette," he would often tell people later.

With the end of track season came the end of his junior year. LaMarr and Victor piloted the mile relay team to a school record and the state finals. The Lettermen's Club voted LaMarr president for the subsequent school year, and he maintained his 4.0/5.0 grade point average.

But the future frightened LaMarr. HK and Victor left for college that summer. Both had received basketball scholarships: Victor to Iowa Wesleyan College and HK to Wyoming along with Coach Bill Purden who accepted a basketball coaching position there. LaMarr's mentors and Thornton's leaders were gone. That left LaMarr and Richie Halbert to fill the voids. LaMarr took his leadership role seriously. The media had aimed a spotlight on him. They predicted that he would break school, state, and national high school football records. They compared him to Gale Sayers. The Illinois press expected the Thornton Wildcats basketball team to win the next state title. Every major college and university wanted LaMarr, but a scholarship depended on his performance, grades, and good health for the 1965-66 school year.

Additionally, he felt pressure at home. Both his siblings, Tina as a freshman and Everett as a sophomore, would be enrolled at Thornton. LaMarr felt protective, and he knew that teachers and students would expect more of them because their big brother had left a large footprint to fill. As freshmen, Tina and Everett followed LaMarr's footsteps in one area - singing. Both had joined the Glee Club. Although Everett was a gifted athlete, he refused to participate on any sports team as a freshman. The burden of being compared to LaMarr was too much for him to bear. LaMarr felt guilty and confronted his younger brother about this. He convinced Everett to join the sophomore football team. "Everett was smart, but he was smaller and lived in LaMarr's shadow. LaMarr always praised and encouraged him," Tina said. The more Clarence recognized the talent of LaMarr, the more he feared that injury, grades, or girls might hinder his son's goal of becoming a college and pro athlete. He could only pray that LaMarr stayed healthy and injury-free, but he made sure LaMarr kept his grades up. Most importantly, he enforced his you-come-home-late-and-the-door-is-locked policy.

LaMarr and Everett started football practice in August. As the grueling two-week pre-season practices progressed, LaMarr accepted his leadership position and its pressures. He joked and sang in the locker room during breaks.

Willie Brown, LaMarr's former coach and academic counselor, stepped to the podium in Thornton's new auditorium/theater. He had been promoted to Dean of Boys, and he addressed an audience of about 700 freshman boys at an orientation the day before the official start of the 1965-66 school year, "I'm Mr. Brown, and my title is Dean of Boys, but I call myself 'Dean of Young Men.' I want to introduce another young man, senior LaMarr Thomas."

LaMarr rose from a metal folding chair behind Willie. He looked like a giant in is his purple and white letterman's sweater with his broad shoulders stretching beyond the dimensions of the lectern. He smiled, shook his head, and said, "Man, I know *exactly* how you feel. Admit it. You are scared to death." He reminisced about how intimidated he was with the size of the new building, the crowded halls, and the fierce competition. He confessed that he let it affect his grades and his attitude during his freshman year. "The remedy," he prescribed, "is getting involved. It doesn't have to be in athletics. It can be clubs, music, theater, anything but gangs."

When he finished, every male freshman wanted to be LaMarr Thomas.

Coach Bauman couldn't have asked for a better start to Wildcat football season. They beat their first two opponents 41-7 and 26-6. LaMarr scored six touchdowns and gained 269 yards. An opposing coach commented on the Thornton team and LaMarr, "A fine, explosive club with perhaps the most explosive halfback in the area and state in LaMarr Thomas."

After five games, LaMarr broke a school record for scoring that had stood for twelve years. In 1953, Brooks Young had scored 73 points. With the win over Lockport 46-0, LaMarr tallied 78 points in a single season.

In the same game, Richie Halbert caught a 28-yard pass that led to a touchdown. Just as the coaches had talked HK into playing football his senior year, they had persuaded Richie Halbert (who also had never played organized football) to join the team as a receiver—again, risky, since he was a three-year varsity basketball star with pending scholarship offers. LaMarr coached Richie on the football fundamentals and vowed to support him just as he had supported HK on the field the previous year.

Coach Bauman's Wildcats ended the 1965 football season undefeated, the first in Thornton's history. The team and LaMarr received local, state, and national recognition. The Press and Radio Association elected LaMarr to both the All-Suburban and All-State first teams. *The Harvey Tribune, The Chicago Sun-Times,* and *The Chicago Daily News* named LaMarr Player of the Year. Jack Jensen, the head

Richie Halbert
Photo courtesy of The Harvey Tribune

sportswriter for *The Harvey Tribune*, reported on the most prestigious award given to a high school football player:

"The most sought-after athlete in the state of Illinois and possibly the Midwest, Thornton's LaMarr Thomas is a member of a high school all-American football team. That honor was bestowed upon him by the publishers of *College and Athlete* magazine. Only 100 athletes in the nation were chosen."

Football season ended, and basketball season had already begun by Thanksgiving of 1965 but not for LaMarr. For the next several weeks, he and Coach Bauman would be speaking and accepting awards from various local and national organizations. New varsity head basketball coach Bob Anderson would have to wait for LaMarr's services, and LaMarr would soon meet with pro football's most valuable player.

LaMarr Thomas
An All-American

Sportswriter Jack Jensen congratulating LaMarr
Photo courtesy of
The Harvey Tribune

Coach Frank Bauman and LaMarr
Photo courtesy of The Harvey Tribune

CHAPTER 9

Sunday, December 12, 1965, 12:06 p.m.

Rain and chilly wind made the turf sloshy and slippery at Wrigley Field where the Chicago Bears played their games. Gale Sayers received a screen pass, sidestepped San Francisco 49ers tacklers, and sprinted eighty yards for a touchdown. He would score five more times in that game to break an NFL record for a single player's touchdowns in one contest.

"I can still see the 49ers sloshing around in the mud," Sayers told the LA Times. "It seemed like everyone was slipping but me."

The feat had added meaning for LaMarr and anyone who had watched him play. The press had been comparing him to Sayers all season. George Halas, Bears owner and head coach, had also been watching LaMarr.

Later that week, the Chicago Bears' front office arranged a meeting with the two halfbacks. A decade later, LaMarr recalled the encounter for the Chicago press:

> "I went to dinner with Gale Sayers after he scored six touchdowns against the 49ers. I thought I wanted to be better than that. I said to myself, 'I'll be better than Sayers when I get to the pros.' I knew I was good."

Gale and LaMarr had more than confidence and football skills in common; they shared a philosophy. "It didn't matter if I scored fifteen touchdowns. Hey, it wouldn't be for me. It would be for the team," Gale told LaMarr and the press.

Football had made LaMarr the most popular student at Thornton. The student body had elected him Homecoming King. "LaMarr had a lot of friends: black, white, old, young, girls, boys, funny, serious. The only thing I can think of that he demanded of his friends was honesty," claimed a boyhood classmate.

The rest of the country was in turmoil. Students on college campuses protested U.S. involvement in the Viet Nam war, and civil rights groups demonstrated and rioted against racism. LaMarr seemed to be ". . . living in a bubble" as Tina Thomas said. "We didn't go through a lot of things other black people went through."

At the same time, subtle racism existed at Thornton Township High School. The demographics of the student body were 20% black, 76% white, and 4% "other," but of the 212 faculty members, 98% were white and 2% black. Willie Brown was the only black participant on the sixteen-member administrative team.

The major sports, football and basketball, consisted of three levels: freshman, sophomore, and varsity. The football program had 170 players, 40% black and 60% white, and ten coaches, nine white and one black. The racial makeup of the basketball players was 60% black and 40% white, but the six-coach staff included only one black coach.

Most high schools, including Thornton, offered few or no girls' competitive sports. Athletic girls could participate in various dance groups, gymnastics club, water ballet, synchronized swimming, GAA (Girls Athletic Association), baton twirling, and cheerleading. Although 50% of the athletes participating in football and basketball were black, all twelve cheerleaders were white.

"The cheerleaders wanted to meet the team; the team wanted to meet the cheerleaders, and not at school," Chris LaVette Thomas said.

After-school get-togethers provided settings for these meetings and led to interracial relationships. LaMarr found a steady girlfriend, and they socialized at these get-togethers and between classes. The girl's parents did not approve of the mixed-race liaison, so the kids kept their relationship secret. Interracial couples were common at Thornton in the 60s; however, many parents, students, and teachers did not accept them.

Rejoining the basketball team curbed LaMarr's social life. "I usually don't let the kids go to dances after the games," Coach Anderson, the new head coach, told the press. Sportswriters picked Thornton to be state champs, and some ranked the team as number one in the country. Anderson felt pressure to succeed and demanded total dedication from his players.

Before LaMarr returned, the team won its first three games and faced its rival, Thornridge. The top scorer in the state, Thornridge's Al Armour, averaged 27.9 points per game. LaMarr, lauded as the top defensive player in the state, guarded him. Thornton won 66-48. When reporters criticized LaMarr for incurring three fouls while guarding Armour, Coach Anderson looked at the scorebook and said, "Well, how many [points] did Armour get—15 is all I see."

The press conference ended.

The Thornton Wildcats lost their first game of the season to Benton High School at the Centralia, Illinois Holiday Tournament finals. Coach Anderson didn't mourn the loss. Instead, he praised both teams for playing a great game. "The free throw line was the ballgame. We played good ball, and we learned." Specifically, LaMarr and Richie Halbert learned a routine. Richie would grab a defensive rebound and LaMarr would fastbreak toward the basket. He would catch a long pass from Richie and score a layup shot. Every opponent after that tournament would have to practice defending "the routine" before playing Thornton.

Photo courtesy of The Harvey Tribune

Sportswriter Jack Jensen had become a staunch promoter/defender of LaMarr. After LaMarr had scored 25 points on January 20th, Jensen devoted an entire column in *The Tribune* to him:

> LaMarr has no problem when it comes to grabbing the attention of the collegiate scouts. In fact, the Wildcat all-stater is in a strong position to pick his spots from a choice that at last count numbered more than 65 major

schools, interested in procuring his talent as a running halfback . . . LaMarr is the finest high school football player people will ever see in these parts. Thomas has to be one of the greatest competitors in athletics ... When Ohio State sticks its head out of the state of Ohio and comes looking, you know how great a player LaMarr Thomas is. The Buckeyes usually have enough talent at home.

College football recruiters, basketball, and schoolwork left little time for LaMarr to spend with his girlfriend, and their relationship deteriorated. He spent his downtime on academics. His love of learning exhibited at Warren Palm rekindled, he was earning 'A's in all his classes including Advanced Placement English IV, Psychology, and U.S. History.

Thornton played Thornridge again, and Ron Ferguson, the Thornridge coach, decided to use LaMarr's defensive skills against the Wildcats. "We didn't want AI [Armour] to get into foul trouble, and we knew that if we kept passing to him, they would kill us because Thomas [LaMarr] is a fabulous defensive player. Anything Al got over 12 tonight was a bonus," Ferguson told the press after Thornridge handed Thornton its second loss, 75-65,

LaMarr sat in the locker room after that game and hung his head. An assistant coach put a towel around LaMarr's neck and said, "Don't feel bad, LaMarr. You did your job. You held Armour who's averaging almost 30 points a game to only 18 points."

Maybe LaMarr recalled Gale Sayers' words to him when he said, "It didn't matter if I held Armour to zero points, Coach. We lost."

Coach Anderson urged the team to "shake off" the loss and turn it into revenge. The regular season was ending and the state playoff series would start. They would meet Thornridge again in the Regional Tournament within weeks. The team took Anderson's words to heart and pulverized their next two opponents.

During a hard practice on the afternoon of Thursday, February 10th, Richie Halbert leaped high and grabbed one of his signature defensive rebounds. LaMarr started the "routine" and raced for a fast break score, but no long pass came to him. A loud scream resonated throughout the gym. Richie had broken his foot; he was out for the season.

The mishap jeopardized Thornton's chances to win a state title again. "The thing we'll miss most from Halbert was his fine defense," Anderson said, but he had a bench full of talent and brought six-foot-three sophomore Herschel Lewis up to the varsity level to compensate for the loss. Coach Anderson's main concern was for Richie. "We'll be weaker without Richie, but I hope his absence the rest of the year won't jeopardize his chance to get a scholarship to college. He can play college basketball. This is a big adjustment for us without Halbert, but Richie probably will have to do more adjusting by being out of action than we'll have to do."

Richie took it hard, and so did LaMarr. As bad as LaMarr felt for the team, he felt worse for Richie. They had become more than teammates; they were friends, and "LaMarr was very sensitive" his wife would often say later. His acute sensitivity and empathy for friends and family affected him. He would get quiet and introspective for days, but find a way to channel his depression into action. He played even harder and became a closer friend to Richie.

"March Madness" for Illinois high school basketball began with the Regional Tournament, and Thornton and Thornridge met in the finals. Thornton took revenge and won 70-45. This time, Coach Anderson didn't assign LaMarr to guard Armour.

Armour scored 20 points, but no other Thornridge players scored in double digits.

Thornton went on to win the sectional and super sectional titles and earned another trip to the Illinois State Basketball Tournament in Champaign. Alec C. Kerr, Chief Editor of *The Harvey Tribune* wrote an editorial on behalf of the publisher and staff:

LAMARR THOMAS JUST HAS TO BE THE GREATEST

One of the greatest thrills we have experienced through this season has been the performance of LAMARR THOMAS who, in our book, ranks with the greatest all-around athletes in the school's history. There could have been, in the course of that history, equally talented football players, and equally talented basketball players, but we cannot remember over some 45 years of observing Thornton teams any single athlete with such a variety of talent.

Thomas, the imperturbable, goes about his athletic chores with the aplomb of a professional. He has the class needed for success in the professional field of sports should he choose that route to fame and fortune, granting, of course, that he first accepts the challenge of a college education which certainly will be made available to him.

Thomas has the speed of a gazelle, the quick moves of a cat, the endurance of an elephant and with all that, the added assets of self-discipline and proper attitude. We have never seen him question a referee's decision, nor have we ever heard him bark at a teammate for a missed play. He is an individual and yet a team man. Above all, he makes few mistakes.

We think it appropriate recognition of this youth's talent that he is an all-stater in his two favorite sports, not to mention All-American in football, in which he attained a pinnacle not even approached by most. We heard a coach remark that he "doesn't have the breakaway speed of BROOKS YOUNG, but he has the maneuvers and desire that make him even more valuable to a team."

We saw him and appreciated him in his football exploits, but we like him even more as a cager. None of the adjectives used by writers and coaches to describe his defensive talent is incorrect. He is in a class by himself in blanketing an opponent with body, arms, hands, and legs. He is a defensive leech in the strictest application of the verbiage and with it all he can contribute liberally on offense when the need for it arises . . .

He is great in every sense of the word.

Even though Jim Ard fouled out and LaMarr committed four fouls, the Thornton Wildcats defeated Galesburg 74-60 on March 19, 1966, and became the Illinois High School State Basketball Champions. Following the game, Sportscaster Vince Lloyd conducted a television interview with the team. Just before asking LaMarr to introduce himself, Lloyd noticed Coach Anderson's eleven-year-old son in the background.

"What are you doing back here, young fella?" Vince asked.

"Nothin," the boy answered.

"What is your name?"

"Dave Anderson."

"And what are you?"

"Mascot."

"And you've been mascot all year?"

"Yes."

"What grade are you in?"

"Fifth."

"How do you feel?"

The boy tried to play off his excitement and said as if he were asked for the time of day, "Pretty good."

The whole team laughed and said, "Come on, Dave."

Lloyd turned his attention to LaMarr who stroked the boy's head, and asked, "LaMarr, what's he supposed to say?"

LaMarr smiled and said in a soft tone that almost sounded like his singing voice, "He feels so-o nice."

The whole team laughed and congratulated LaMarr for verbalizing their emotions. All the Illinois newspapers picked up on the line and headlines read: IT FEELS SO NICE.

The next day, Sunday, 15,000 people packed inside and outside the Thornton gymnasium to greet and to honor the team. The crowd demanded LaMarr speak at the stage podium. He stepped up to the microphone and gazed at the hushed audience. This was the pinnacle of his life as a teen. Growing up in Markham, developing a love of learning at Warren Palm, singing in church and on team busses, running for touchdowns, blocking shots, and scoring baskets were among "the bubble" within which he lived.

"I feel so-o nice," he said in his musical voice.

Fifteen thousand people rose and screamed with joy.

The bubble would soon burst.

PART 2:
BURSTING THE BUBBLE

CHAPTER 10

March 31, 1966

East Lansing, Michigan

Duffy Daugherty put his hands behind his head and sat back in his cushioned leather chair. His Michigan State University football team would start spring practice in less than a month, and he hadn't signed all his new players. On his desktop lay the four-year scholarship contract for LaMarr Thomas, unsigned. Duffy worried, but he wasn't surprised. LaMarr had over 70 scholarship offers, and he had been too busy helping his high school basketball team win a state championship to vet all his opportunities.

The many trophies, plaques, and awards of MSU's football team over the decades were shelved behind Head Coach Daugherty's desk—most recently, the College Football National Championship trophy. His personal accolades included the Eddie Robinson Coach of the Year plaque awarded by the Football Writers' Association of America in 1965 and a team picture of the 1939 Syracuse "Orange" football team on which Duffy had played guard and served as team captain.

The team picture foreshadowed Duffy's reputation for recruiting black football players. He had played with the first black college football player, Wilmeth Sidat-Singh. Most college teams' policies forbade them from playing other teams with black players, so Syracuse listed him as being of Indian descent. Sportswriters dubbed Duffy's recruiting method as "The Underground Railroad" because he lured black players from southern high schools, particularly in Texas and the Carolinas. Duffy scoffed at his critics who said he was exploiting poor black kids who didn't deserve college educations.

"They used to say I was getting the black kids who were poor students, but I have my doctors and lawyers," he said. "I'm not proud of them because they were black. Instead, it is because by their success, they refuted the bigots who said they were not intelligent."

John Matthews Smith, in his 2007 article "Breaking the Plane," described how Duffy handled his critics:

> A number of alumni questioned why he used so many black players. He recalled one alumni meeting where in the middle of his speech someone yelled, "Hey, Duf, how many niggers are you gonna start this year?" Duffy responded by questioning the manhood of the racist who was willing to yell an epithet from the back of the room but unwilling to step forward, identify himself, and take responsibility for his words. The room fell silent. Daugherty explained that it was his policy to "play the best players whether they happened to be all black or all white." At another gathering at another alumnus's home, a man threatened the coach, "Duffy, you've been starting a lot of niggers lately. You know the minute you start four of five in the backfield, you've lost me." Daugherty looked the man straight in the eye and said, "Then, I've lost you right now," and with that he left.

Clinton Jones, Bob Apisa, Bubba Smith, Gene Washington, George Webster, and Duffy Daughterty

Photo courtesy of Michigan State University

Duffy had committed to starting Jimmy Raye as his quarterback, one of the few black quarterbacks playing in Division I football at that time. He also wanted one of the best high school running backs in his backfield. Whoever he acquired would have to sit out college varsity football his freshman year, an NCAA rule back then, but Duffy was willing to groom the best for the future.

He sat forward and picked up the scholarship document with LaMarr's name on it.

"I've got to sign this kid," he said.

That same night, LaMarr would be honored at a banquet sponsored by the Suburban Press and Radio Association for being selected as the Best All-Around Athlete in Illinois, but he wasn't thinking about his many honors and awards. He was thinking about his future. The immediate future included a family trip that weekend to Michigan State University, compliments of Duffy Daugherty and the MSU Athletic Department.

"We stayed at Duffy's house," Tina Thomas recalled. "They treated us like royalty."

LaMarr's personal tour guide was All-American defensive end Bubba Smith. Bubba would later become an NFL star with the Baltimore Colts, the Oakland Raiders, and the Houston Oilers, before his television and movie acting career.

Bubba drove LaMarr down Shaw Lane and turned into the stadium parking lot. The MSU student body referred to Bubba's flashy Cadillac as the "Bubba-mobile." They walked through the stadium and into the training rooms and locker room facilities. He showed LaMarr the academic and administrative buildings. A long line of students waited to enter a building.

"What's that about?" LaMarr asked.

"They're registering for fall classes," Bubba said. "Don't worry about that. Assistant coaches take care of all that for us."

"So why did you choose MSU?" LaMarr asked.

"I wanted to sign with the University of Texas and be close to home, but UT doesn't offer scholarships to negroes. Duffy's different. We've got more black brothers on this team than any other Big Ten school, and they treat us okay, better than they do in Texas anyway."

"What's Texas like?"

"The real world," Bubba said, and they headed back toward Duffy's house.

CHAPTER 11

Easter Sunday, April 10, 1966

Chicago newspapers and suburban presses carried the same sports page headline: LAMARR CHOOSES MICHIGAN STATE. In an exclusive interview with *The Harvey Tribune*, LaMarr revealed his reasons for choosing MSU. "When I got to East Lansing, that was it. The campus, some of the students and the townspeople . . . they all impressed me so much. Everyone at Michigan State seemed genuinely interested in me, whether I was a football recruit or not." He said that he wanted to enroll in the School of Business, majoring in accounting and minoring in history. "I've thought about coaching, but professional football has always been my first real dream. I don't know if I have the patience for coaching, but I do like to work with figures."

Signing with Michigan State meant that no other Big 10 school could continue to recruit him; however, NCAA rules allowed schools from other conferences to try and lure LaMarr away from MSU. Consequently, MSU, as well as other Big 10 schools, continued to "wine and dine" inside (and sometimes outside) the NCAA rules and guidelines.

"We'll take care of you." Tina Thomas recalled either MSU athletic department personnel or alumni telling her family. "They gave us money. Not LaMarr, but they gave our parents money."

Clarence (father), LaMarr, and Frances (mother) discuss MSU
scholarship signing
Photo courtesy of The Harvey Tribune

The school year would end in two months, but in LaMarr's mind, Thornton Township High School was already in his rearview mirror. "The spirit of Thornton, the winning attitude, and the unselfish group of players we had this year in football and basketball I will always remember. I don't know what it is at Thornton, the keen attitude to win or the pride, but I've had some fine associations here. The whole athletic season I will remember, not just one special game."

Prior to signing with MSU and becoming center focus of the sports press, LaMarr had decided to end his athletic career at TTHS by playing baseball, to the dismay of the head track coach, Bill Hayes, "LaMarr Thomas, a [state qualifying] mile relay team member last year, has reported for baseball this spring."

However, the headlines made LaMarr a statewide celebrity and he didn't have time to play baseball. Community organizations called upon him to deliver speeches and to accept and give out civic awards.

He finished high school with a 4.8/5.0 grade point average with his last "free" summer ahead. Aspirations of college and professional football meant spring and summer practices for years to come. Since MSU freshman football training wouldn't start until late summer and his four-year scholarship included room, board, tuition, and books, LaMarr didn't need to get a summer job; he took full advantage of attending post-graduation parties and enjoyed the summer.

Richie Halbert never got over missing the state championship, but he also didn't forget the support and friendship LaMarr provided him. As a common friend to Chris LaVette and LaMarr, he played matchmaker. He knew that the former cheerleader and athletic star shared a mutual attraction throughout their senior year, but each felt committed to separate relationships.

Chris recalled, "I remember Richie calling me and saying, 'Come to a party. LaMarr will be there.' LaMarr and I talked, and that's where it all started. My stepfather was a fan and asked if I wanted to invite some of LaMarr's and my friends for dinner." LaMarr and Chris dated throughout the summer.

When not with Chris, LaMarr devoted his time to family and friends. Clarence, Frances, Everett, and Tina cherished the time LaMarr spent at family cookouts and gatherings. Victor and HK, home from their respective colleges, partied and played basketball with LaMarr and his friends including Richie Halbert. Despite Richie's missing most of the previous basketball season and Coach Anderson's worry about that jeopardizing his chances to play college ball, Richie received a four-year basketball scholarship to Cornell College in Mount Vernon, Iowa. Overall, the summer of 1966 might have been LaMarr's most memorable vacation time as a teenager, but it had to come to a bittersweet end. He would be leaving for East Lansing, Michigan in August while Chris stayed in the Chicago area to attend Roosevelt University.

A week before leaving, LaMarr received his class schedule in the mail. He had met with an MSU academic advisor that summer to discuss his educational goals and first year course selections. Bubba Smith had told him that following the advisor/student meeting, assistant football coaches would take care of registering him for his classes. He recognized some of the core courses, English 111 and Natural Science 181, that he had agreed to take; however, he wondered who added Foundations of Physical Ed. 105, Football 307, and Advanced Football 421 and how these courses would lead to a degree in business or history.

He folded the schedule and began to pack.

CHAPTER 12

September 1966

Bubba Smith, LaMarr, and a few other MSU football players remained in the shower room adjacent to the locker room after a long practice in the hot sun. With soapy water clinging to his chest hairs, Bubba walked in front of LaMarr. Using his fingertips, he flung the wet suds into LaMarr eyes. LaMarr rubbed his eyes with water until the burning stopped then pushed his palm under Bubba's chin and forced him against the wall.

"No one treats me like that—not even the *great* Bubba Smith," LaMarr said and dropped his hand.

Bubba smiled, nodded his head, and walked away.

At 9:10 a.m. on November 18th 1966, thousands of students chanted, "Kill, Bubba, Kill!" outside of All-American defensive end Bubba Smith's window at Wonders Hall on Michigan State's campus. The following day, Bubba and the Number 2 ranked MSU football team would play in what the sports world called "The Game of the Century" against Number 1 ranked Notre Dame.

The night before the game, Bubba cruised around East Lansing, Michigan in his "Bubba-mobile" when police arrested him for a traffic violation and put him jail for several outstanding traffic warrants. Bubba, who often talked about himself in third person, said, "Man, there ain't no way they're going to arrest Bubba Smith," and he was right. MSU Athletic Director Biggie Mann got Bubba out of jail and threatened the Chief of Police.

Millions watched the game on ABC national television, and soldiers in Viet Nam could view it via satellite. The Nielsen Television Ratings for that game steeped higher than the ratings for the first Super Bowl the following year.

The game ended in a tie, 10-10. The controversy over who was Number 1 remained unresolved. When asked how he felt about the game, Duffy allegedly replied, "A tie is like kissing your sister."

LaMarr and the other freshman football players watched the game from the stands with tens of thousands of spectators because only varsity players could be on the sidelines; however, Duffy had not forgotten his frosh players. Within days of the end of the college football season, his thoughts turned to the future. He reviewed the report from freshman football coach Ed Rutherford. The report praised LaMarr, not only for his physical

Ara Parseghian and Duffy Daugherty after "The Game of the Century"
Photo courtesy of Associated Press

Dr. Martin Luther King and Dr. Robert Green at a Press Conference
Photo courtesy of Robert L. Green & Associates

football talent, but also for his mental brightness and quick learning skills. Duffy scanned LaMarr's first quarter academic grades—practically all 'A's and 'B's.

It was time to call Dr. Green.

Robert L. Green had been affiliated with MSU since 1960. He received his Ph.D. in Educational Psychology from MSU and was a nationally known scholar and an expert on education, urban development, and diversity issues. Since 1965, Dr. Martin Luther King had employed him as the Education Director for the Southern Christian Leadership Conference, but his primary position was that of professor at Michigan State University.

Unofficially, Dr. Green was much more at MSU, as he explained in his book *At the Crossroads of Fear and Freedom*:

> I was an unpaid recruiter and counselor to many
> black student-athletes. Working with Duffy, who had
> a green light from President Hannah, we created an

Underground Railroad for southern black athletes. Black football players confided in me because I helped recruit some of them. Lettie [Dr. Green's wife] and I often hosted student-athletes at our home for food and talk. They sometimes visited without invitation.

"I have a really good ballplayer," Duffy told Dr. Green, "But more than that he's a good student as well and any support you can give would be really appreciated."

On a cold, blustery February day in 1967, LaMarr knocked on the door of the Greens' home in East Lansing, Michigan. Lettie answered the door, and LaMarr explained that Dr. Green had invited him to meet with him and other Michigan State students. Lettie escorted him to the basement where Dr. Green had set up a conference area.

Dr. Green and a half-dozen students engaged in lively conversation. As LaMarr descended the stairs, the discussion ceased, and all eyes looked up at him. Dr. Green introduced him to the group which included Jason LaVette, Barry Amos, and Richard Thomas. The spirited discussion returned to topics such as segregated housing on campus and the nation, unequal pay for black workers, discrimination in hiring, and racist remarks.

LaMarr sat back and listened. The scholarly discourse amazed him. These weren't enraged radical rebels complaining. These were bright students exploring problems with intellectual insights, theories, and solutions.

That night, as he lay awake in his dorm room, his head swam with thoughts. Questions haunted him: Why were there so many black athletes at MSU and no black coaches? Why were black athletes encouraged to take unchallenging classes that didn't lead to degrees? Why, if segregation was illegal, was there all-black housing on campus and in East Lansing? Were these solely Michigan State University problems or reflections of nationwide discrimination and racism?

The more LaMarr attended these sessions at Dr. Green's home, the more enlightened he became about the "real world" Bubba Smith had mentioned during his orientation days six months earlier. He participated more in the discussions and bonded with Richard Thomas.

Richard Thomas reading poetry on the MSU campus circa late 1960s
Photo courtesy of Richard Thomas

Richard, an ex-Marine, had grown up in Detroit where racial tensions had heated up during the 1960s. Discrimination and segregation led to protests and riots. He had experienced the racial turmoil that the Thomas family had fled from when they moved to the suburbs. LaMarr had never met anyone like Richard, a strong, young black man who was also a scholar and a poet. His poetry earned praise from renowned poet Langston Hughes and poet/playwright Leroi Jones. Richard recalled, "LaMarr and I became interested in the black student movement at the same time. Some of us had met at Dr. Green's house, and we were in some history classes together. Dr. Green wanted to know why we hadn't started a black student union, and right then we started one."

With Dr. Green's guidance, this small black student union began addressing the issues they had discussed. "I never advised them [MSU black students] to take things lying down. If you saw injustice, you stood up," Dr. Green had said. His close association with Martin Luther King Jr. gave the group a lens through which to observe national racial issues such as a fair housing campaign in Milwaukee led by the NAACP Youth Council and a Supreme Court case involving a law banning interracial marriages in Virginia. The group constructed and sent letters and petitions of support or opposition to the leaders involved in these matters, but their influence was minimal.

They needed a clear vision and a name for their organization. The Black Panthers Party had evolved into a Marxist revolutionary group with a vision that involved the arming of all African Americans. Dr. King envisioned "a world where his children would not be judged by the color of their skin, but by the content of their character" through nonviolent protest. Malcolm X's Nation of Islam envisioned black nationalism as the path to social justice.

To clarify the group's vision and focus, LaMarr, Richard, and the other members who met with Dr. Green studied the existing black movements. Their research came to a climax in the spring of 1967 when Robert Little, brother of assassinated Malcom X, came to MSU and gave a fiery speech advocating black nationalism. In *At the Crossroads of Fear and Freedom*, Dr. Green described what had happened:

> As he [Robert Little] moved to his closing comments, he looked directly at me and criticized me for "opposing" the black nationalism espoused by his brother. There was silence as everyone in the room turned and looked at me. I stood up to respond.
>
> I then looked around the room at some of the students—Richard Thomas, Jason LaVette, Barry Amos, and LaMarr Thomas. I pointed to each of them as I continued, "And to you, Richard, and to you Jason, and to you Barry, and to you LaMarr," I said, "to any of you who say you believe in black nationalism, I accuse you of being hypocrites for being here on this

white campus, rather than out on the streets putting your lives on the line, like Malcolm X did; like Martin Luther King, Andrew Young, and Stokely Carmichael are doing this very moment!"

After chastising the students, I complimented them for being socially conscious and active and reminded [the audience] that young people and their organizations were making a difference.

Dr. Green's admonition had helped them discover their vision and focus. They would fight for social justice and civil rights within the parameters of integration and peaceful protest. As the 1966-67 school term ended, naming their group would have to wait for the fall semester.

Meanwhile, LaMarr's name hit the Chicago press again. The big news in Illinois was a slush fund scandal involving coaches and players at the University of Illinois that led to several resignations and players losing their scholarships. The state senate, led by Senator Everett Peters, established a committee to investigate Big 10 schools' recruiting methods. Speaking to the press, Peters said, "Remember, we can subpoena anyone in the state and that includes Bill Reed [Big 10 Commissioner]. We can put our own players on the stand, and we can catch plenty of Big Ten athletes when they come home, like LaMarr Thomas of Markham, now a freshman star at Michigan State. We can put them under oath, and if they take the Fifth Amendment that will be even more incriminating. If things get hot enough, the seal will break someplace."

Sportswriter Jack Jensen, who had praised LaMarr during his high school years, rallied to his defense. "Thomas is a fine, upstanding young man from a fine family. LaMarr, in our estimation, would never take any special gift from any particular school to sign a tender with that institution, even if it was offered. And in his case, it wasn't. Thomas is a big-time athlete in every way, but even better, he's a big-time person off the floor or the field. He's one of the finest young men it has been anybody's pleasure to meet, to converse or undoubtedly to coach. It seems poor to even link him with slush money."

Senator Peters' constituency warned him that going after statewide icon LaMarr Thomas might have political consequences, and the committee backed off. Nevertheless, LaMarr did not return to Markham for one of his frequent weekend visits to see his family and girlfriend, Chris. He reported directly to spring football training in April.

The spring term ended in June, and Richard Thomas boarded a Greyhound bus for home. He would face what historians deemed "The Long Hot Summer" of violence and race riots in Detroit. As many MSU undergrads headed home, LaMarr lay in his dorm room contemplating a new dilemma. He had lived by his own words to younger brother Everett, "You always have to do what's best for the team, not just what's best for you." As a kid and a teenager, LaMarr found it easy to live by those words. First, he discovered that what was good for the team was also good for him. It brought him fame, friends, and a free ride to college. Second, he separated his team loyalty. In the fall, he was loyal to his football team. In the winter, he pledged his loyalty to his basketball team. When not playing sports and during the off-seasons, he focused on family and friends.

But now, he found himself on two teams, simultaneously—the Michigan State University football team and the black student union. If the two conflicted, could he be loyal to both? His childhood Bible studies told him, "No one can serve two masters, for either he will hate the one and love the other, or he will be devoted to one and despise the other."

He grabbed his football spikes and went to practice.

CHAPTER 13

Summer, 1967

From the collected poems and narratives, *Richard W Thomas Going Home to My Soul*:

> I returned from Michigan State University, and Detroit was still burning. Troops and tanks were in the streets. I was stopped by National Guardsmen as I left the Greyhound bus station, but I made it home. Many local groceries and supermarkets closed during this time. My father and I had to leave our neighborhood to find food. Some white dudes in a car yelled racial epithets at us. My father, never one to back down, yelled back. Rumors were constantly circulating about "the next hot summer." Concerned about my parents and sister in what was quickly becoming a "food desert," I started storing food in their house just in case another riot/rebellion broke out, and they might be forced to go into hostile white neighborhoods to get food. At the time, there was talk in the white media and among people I knew that Blacks were burning their own neighborhoods.

Ninety miles away in East Lansing, LaMarr was working hard on the gridiron to secure a starting position in the MSU football team's backfield. Although too busy to focus on the Detroit turmoil and the 159 race riots erupting in big cities nationwide, he was now more aware of discriminatory practices around him. He wondered why MSU was number one in the Big 10 for recruiting black football players, but number ten at hiring black coaches. All the athletic department support staff (workers in the Jenison fieldhouse, the intramural building, the ticket office, and ice arena) were white. Blacks represented fifteen percent of major league baseball players, but MSU had not recruited a single black high school player. Guidance counselors steered black players toward unchallenging courses that assured academic eligibility but did not lead to diplomas. As of 1967, no black woman had ever been selected for the cheerleading squad.

LaMarr shared his concerns with fellow teammates, black and white. A substantial number of black players agreed that something needed to be done about the inequities. A smaller number thought he should "leave well enough alone" and just concentrate on football. If any of the white players agreed with LaMarr, they didn't let him know it. One white player and an assistant coach privately referred to him as the "uppity nigger."

Richard and thousands of MSU students returned to East Lansing during the second week of September for the fall term. That Saturday, LaMarr, Richard, and a dozen or so other black students met at Dr. Green's home and established a name for their organization, as explained on their current website:

> Black Students' Alliance was founded on September 9, 1967, in the basement of Dr. Robert L. Green's home. This organization was created at the time of student protests surrounding racism on MSU's campus. Dr. Green's basement served as a space for this organization to organize and plan as the central advocacy group for Black students on campus. To

this day, Black Student Alliance remains the voice of Black students on campus. We are your advocates, confidants, and support system. Black Student Alliance ensures your voice is heard.

More than creating a name, the Black Students' Alliance (BSA) reviewed grievances and injustices occurring nationally and locally. LaMarr became the spokesperson for concerns on campus and, more specifically, within athletics. Richard and other members shared problems existing in their hometowns. Dr. Green's affiliation with Dr. King and other national groups showed the BSA how their concerns fit within the context of nationwide problems. Moreover, they agreed that action needed to be taken. The questions were: What actions and when?

Two weeks from that Saturday, the MSU Spartans would take the football field for the first game of the season. The AP press polls ranked the Spartans third in the nation, and Duffy Daugherty reported on his starting backfield, "Junior Frank Waters and sophomore LaMarr Thomas are candidates for the other halfback. Right now, Waters has the edge." Even if Duffy had chosen the more seasoned player, Waters, as his starting running back, he couldn't ignore LaMarr's stellar talent and assured him substantial playing time.

LaMarr found himself on two teams: the MSU football team and the Black Students' Alliance. On one, he was fighting for a winning season. On the other, he was fighting for black human rights, black student rights and, more specifically, black student-athlete rights. He had decided to "serve two masters" and battle for both teams.

LaMarr's parents, Clarence and Frances, and girlfriend Chris LaVette traveled to East Lansing for the first game against Houston University. Chris and LaMarr dated whenever he could travel home during the 1966-67 school year. They also communicated through letters.

Unfortunately, the MSU Spartans lost their first two games and fell out of the national rankings. LaMarr provided the only bright spots. In the first game against Houston, he ran for a 48-yard touchdown in the first quarter for the Spartan's only score in a 37-7 loss. In the second loss to Number 2 ranked USC 21-17, LaMarr racked up more yardage, but USC's O.J. Simpson dominated the game by rushing for 190 yards.

Sportswriters blamed MSU's losses on Duffy for not playing LaMarr enough:

> *Benton Harbor New Palladium* October 5, 1967
> Reserve halfback LaMarr Thomas is being groomed for duty against Wisconsin. So far, he has carried the ball only eight times, but has gained 81 yards and scored a touchdown on a 48-yard run.

Duffy recognized his mistake in not starting LaMarr and giving him more playing time. Before the third game against Wisconsin, John Coatta, the Badgers head coach, acknowledged LaMarr's talent. "Sophomore halfback LaMarr Thomas and quarterback Jimmy Raye concern me. Thomas is big and fast, and Raye is extremely quick and can throw."

Coatta was right to worry about LaMarr. As the starting halfback, his performance against Wisconsin might have been the most impressive of his college football career. LaMarr picked up 106 yards in fourteen carries, ran for one touchdown, and passed for a 44-yard touchdown halfback option play. His rushing average of 8.5 yards per carry exceeded that of all starting halfbacks in the Big 10. MSU beat Wisconsin 35-7.

The campus fame and media attention he had enjoyed at Thornton High School returned to him at Michigan State University. Since LaMarr's high school days, the press and Chicago Bears head coach George Halas had compared him to

Gale Sayers. Halas retired as head coach after the 1967 season but remained owner of the Bears. LaMarr would become eligible for the NFL draft after 1969. At that time, Sayers would have played five years for the Bears and would be twenty-six years old. Halas made no secret that he wanted to draft LaMarr and was willing to sacrifice future draft picks for the chance.

The next week, the Spartans trounced rival Michigan 34-0 but lost their fifth game to Minnesota 17-0. Their next opponent would be Notre Dame, and Duffy wanted revenge. Even though last year's "Game of the Century" had ended in a tie, many sportswriters labeled Notre Dame number one and MSU number two.

LaMarr awoke at 5 a.m. on October 23rd and prepared for a typical Monday-after-a-Saturday-game: 5-6:30 a.m., pack for the day and eat breakfast; 6:45-8 a.m., strength and conditioning; 8-8:30 a.m., shower and get to classes; 9 a.m.-2 p.m., classes and lunch; 2:30-3:15 p.m., review film of the previous game before practice at 3:30 p.m.

Loud conversations erupted inside the film room as players waited for Duffy to arrive and to "break down" the mistakes made in the Minnesota game. Duffy arrived followed by assistant coaches. The players took their seats and the talking ceased. As Duffy addressed them, an assistant coach entered and handed LaMarr a note. LaMarr read the note, grabbed his books, and dashed out.

"What's that about?" asked Duffy.

A player seated near LaMarr picked up the note on the floor and read it. He looked up and said, "It's from the RA [Resident Advisor] at his dorm. It says that some guy named Rich Halbert died in a car crash."

The silence continued.

CHAPTER 14

October 26, 1967

Late that afternoon, LaMarr boarded a bus at the Lansing Greyhound station bound for Chicago. Duffy had excused him from Friday's pre-game practice to attend Richie's funeral. He was still in shock. He had called home from his dorm after leaving the film room. Whoever answered confirmed the shocking news, but no one knew the details. Between classes that week he visited the MSU Library and obtained an Associated Press clipping from a Cedar Rapids, Iowa newspaper:

> A student at Cornell College in Mount Vernon,
> Richard Halbert, 19, of Harvey, Illinois, was killed
> when the car in which he was riding slammed into a
> culvert on a county road east of Cedar Rapids …

Even after reading the article, he was in disbelief. He practiced hard Tuesday through Thursday for the Notre Dame game but couldn't keep his mind off Richie's death.

He sat in his bus seat, closed his eyes, and tried to sleep. He dreamed of playing basketball with Richie and executing "the routine"—Richie grabbing a defensive rebound, LaMarr breaking for the basket, when suddenly screams emanated from within a mangled car in a ditch. LaMarr awakened as if someone had slapped him and wondered if he had screamed out loud, but the other passengers didn't seemed startled. He touched his face. It was wet from tears.

Friday morning, LaMarr, Jim Ard, Richard Rateree, and other members of the 1966 Thornton state championship basketball team sat together at Daniel Chapel Zion Church in Phoenix, Illinois for Richie's funeral services. The packed church included people from the Chicago area and Mount Vernon, Iowa where Richie attended Cornell College and would have been a basketball starter as a sophomore. Forty members of Richie's fraternity traveled from Iowa to attend the funeral. Among the speakers delivering eulogies was Dean Stuart Good, Dean of Student Affairs at Cornell who explained that 600 students attended a memorial service at King Chapel on campus to honor Richie. As the organ played and the congregation followed the casket down the aisle, out the doors, and into the hearse, reality hit LaMarr and the other young men seated with him. It didn't matter that Richie had been a champion, won a scholarship, and earned a place on a college varsity team. It didn't matter that he was young with a bright future. Death doesn't care and can come at any time.

"It's not fair. It's not right," LaMarr complained to family and friends before returning to MSU that night, but no one had any answers for him. Even though he had a big game the next day, he stayed awake all night on the bus. He was emotionally exhausted but his thoughts raced of the Notre Dame game, classes, the Black Students' Alliance, football, family, friends, the future.

On Saturday morning, LaMarr caught the team bus bound for South Bend, Indiana. Because the Greyhound bus from Chicago had pulled into Lansing late Friday night, LaMarr didn't get to his dorm room until after midnight. Unlike his six teammates, he had a legitimate excuse for breaking the Duffy Daugherty curfew rule for his players. Duffy suspended all six players which included four starters for the Notre Dame game. Quarterback Jimmy Raye was sidelined with bruised ribs. In the third quarter, LaMarr fumbled on the Irish 18-yardline, and the Spartans lost 24-12. "Your head was not in the game" an assistant coach told LaMarr after the game.

The week had been a disaster for LaMarr, but when he awoke Sunday morning, October 29th, everything seemed to come together. Richie's death had taught him about the brevity of life and the need for immediate action. His concept of putting his team first had been easy to implement when he a boy but more complicated to apply as an adult. As a child, he could separate his team loyalties. As a young man, he found himself on several teams at once and his loyalties were conflicted. On the football team, he a was warrior with a mission to win each Saturday and bring pride and money to his school. In return, he would bring pride and money to himself if drafted into the pros. As a member of the Black Students' Alliance, he was on a team of scholars fighting against discrimination and racial injustice within society. He recognized those social biases and inequities inherent within the MSU campus, the athletic department, and the football team.

"How can I serve two masters?"

He contemplated a solution and took it to his mentor that Sunday evening.

In Dr. Green's conference room at his home, he and LaMarr sat and faced each other. LaMarr leaned forward and fumbled for the right words before blurting, "I'm thinking of quitting football. I think I'm going to spend my time being a scholar."

"It was the one time he truly surprised me," Dr. Green recalled later.

LaMarr explained that he felt like he was wasting his life playing a game when he could be studying the world and ways to make it better. Dr. Green agreed but played the devil's advocate to help LaMarr evaluate his decision.

"Can't you do both?"

"I don't think so," LaMarr countered. "Football demands a lot of time and energy—time and energy that can be better spent helping solve important problems."

"As a famous and rich football player you'd have a louder voice, a bigger audience, and money to help causes."

"Yes, but a football player is a jock, not a scholar. His knowledge and his opinions lack authority because he's focused his limited time on earth perfecting his body and talent and not his mind."

Dr. Green presented his final argument, "Fine, LaMarr, but a lot of people are going to be upset."

LaMarr hung his head. He had no answer for that one, and it plagued his decision. He thought about Duffy. He genuinely liked Duffy and appreciated all he had done for him. His teammates depended on him and his talents. Finally, he thought about his family and friends, particularly his father. The dream of playing pro football may have been fading in LaMarr's mind, but it still burned in Clarence's heart. Would his friends understand? Would they still support and love him if he quit football?

As LaMarr prepared to leave, Dr. Green offered his final advice, "You have to do what's best for LaMarr."

The next morning, LaMarr showed up for strength and conditioning. He had made a short-termed decision. He would finish the football season; he never considered himself a quitter. After the season, he would further ponder whether to leave football and follow the road of a scholar/activist. In the meantime, he would "serve two masters": The Michigan State University Spartan Football Team and the Black Students' Alliance. When not practicing or playing football, he met with his BSA friends and discussed social and racial issues.

The 1967 football season proved to be the worst for Duffy and the Spartans. Their last four games were against Big 10 Conference teams; they lost three. The first loss to Ohio State gave Buckeyes' head coach, Woody Hayes, special pleasure. He had tried unsuccessfully to lure LaMarr to Ohio State. Woody knew that LaMarr led the Big 10 starting halfbacks by averaging five yards rushing per carry. Woody cheered when Duffy gambled, and LaMarr failed to make a first down on a fourth-down play. After losing to Ohio State 21-7, the Spartans faced Indiana and lost again 14-13. Number 10 ranked Purdue beat them 21-7, but every newspaper covering the game noted how LaMarr's and Regis Cavender's efforts nearly turned the game around:

> A pair of last-minute tackles prevented both LaMarr Thomas and Regis Cavender from scoring on long distance runs.

During this three-week period before the final conference game against Northwestern, LaMarr and the BSA had been exploring racial discrimination on the MSU campus and nationwide. Although the Civil Rights Act of 1964 supposedly ended segregation in public places and banned hiring prejudice, racist practices continued in the United States, including at Michigan State University. Despite MSU eliminating the question of race on admission applications, housing applications required a photo, and black students tended to get black roommates in predominately black-populated dorms. In 1967, all administrators, college deans, and counselors were white. The university had employed only four black faculty members.

Racial inequities glowed brightest in the Athletic Department. One discriminatory practice unique to athletics was "stacking." Benjamin Paul Phillips, in his 2015 dissertation *All-American Activism* defined the term, "This was a strategy of grouping many African-American athletes together at one position, often running back, wide receiver, or cornerback, a practice that many black players felt led to the inevitability of more white players being starters at other positions."

LaMarr became the BSA spokesperson for all MSU sports. He rallied several black football players around these concerns, but this excluded him from the social camaraderie enjoyed by many of the players. Charles Bailey, teammate and All-Big 10 Conference defensive tackle, explained. "LaMarr was a very serious type of guy. It seems like the civil rights movement really changed his attitude about a lot of things. He wasn't the same after that. He really didn't hang out with a lot of the guys like a lot of us hung out together and went to parties. LaMarr never really was in that scene. He was always sort of off to himself. Good guy though. He was a unique guy, not the average guy."

The BSA encouraged LaMarr to organize a team boycott of the final MSU football game with Northwestern University; however, cooler heads prevailed and the idea was vetoed. One reason—the Spartans' dismal season made losing or winning the game meaningless. No bowl game or conference championship was at stake. A loss would have handed Duffy his worst season record as a head coach. Even those players who felt Duffy was responsible for some discriminatory concerns respected him and didn't think he deserved that distinction. The major reason for the cancellation involved organization. A boycott involving more athletes from other sports and a list of specific demands and remedies would be more effective, so the idea was tabled.

MSU's 41-27 victory over Northwestern left them with a 3-7 season record, the Spartans' worst in fifty years. Duffy stuck to tradition and had played as many upperclassmen as possible in the season finale, so LaMarr's playing time was minimal; however, Duffy praised him when he prophesized a great 1968 season, "Just look at LaMarr's stats and tell me he . . . we won't be great." Even though Duffy didn't start him every game and often played the more seasoned senior, Dwight Lee, LaMarr racked up 311 rushing yards in 74 attempts—second only to Lee's 497 yards in 116 attempts. LaMarr averaged 4.2 yards per carry, eighth-highest among all Big 10 players. Lee went on to play for the San Francisco 49ers and the Atlanta Falcons.

Playing football, attending classes, and taking an active role in the Black Students' Alliance exhausted LaMarr. He looked forward to going home for the holidays after the fall term, but he also felt trepidation. He hadn't decided about his future. Should he quit football and devote his time to becoming a scholar and an activist? Should he try to do both? Could he do both? So far, he had only shared his dilemma with Dr. Green and a few confidantes. Whatever his decision, it would affect others: Duffy, his football team, the BSA, his friends, and most importantly, his family.

He would have to share his thoughts with family; Clarence would not be pleased.

LaMarr packed his bags and headed to the bus station.

CHAPTER 15

"Go ahead and fight for those things, but if you stay in football and become a pro, you'll have a higher platform." Clarence said as he leaned over the kitchen table to speak to LaMarr.

LaMarr stared right back at his father. He didn't look down in shame like when he was a boy; it was man-to-man now. LaMarr had picked this day between Christmas and New Year's Day (traditionally a joyous time at the Thomas home in Markham, Illinois) to share his thoughts about quitting football and becoming a scholar/activist for civil rights.

Harry Oryhon, LaMarr's boyhood friend from Warren Palm Elementary, sat at the table with them. "Play the 'f-ing' game. You'll be so good. The doors will be open to you," Harry pleaded.

"Money talks," Clarence added.

LaMarr stopped arguing. He decided to give football at least another year and "serve two masters;" however, he had changed his mind about his academic direction. Previously, his course load consisted of basic business classes and football related curricula. For the winter term of his sophomore year, he had registered for Introduction to Social Science, Contemporary Social Problems, and Collective Behavior.

He also decided to become a more active member of the Black Students' Alliance. While at home during the Christmas/

New Year break, he discussed this decision with his girlfriend, Chris. They concurred that the optics of LaMarr with a white girlfriend might discredit his position as an activist fighting for black students' causes. They agreed to suspend their relationship and date other people.

When LaMarr returned to MSU in January of 1968, civil unrest brewed on college campuses across the country. Students protested many issues - the war in Viet Nam, poverty, racism, women's inequality, and unemployment. A national organization of college students formed, Students for a Democratic Society (SDS), as an umbrella encompassing social complaints. Barry Amis, the first president of the Black Students' Alliance at MSU explained, "It [SDS] had taken over buildings at schools (Columbia University, Wisconsin, and a few other places) and basically trashed them. That was the radical extremism of the left. Some students wanted to emulate that. We [BSA] didn't." Following the example of Dr. Green who followed the example of Martin Luther King Jr., the organization was about standing up to injustices using nonviolent means.

LaMarr talked with black student/athletes and collected complaints and concerns. He wasn't shy about voicing his findings on campus, and the press often quoted him:

> LaMarr Thomas, the student athlete representative for the football players, argued that there was a feeling that black athletes were being "messed over" by the athletic department and were treated largely as "black stock" by the university. In short, they felt "used" by a system that benefited greatly from their athletic prowess and the positive press that they generated, but cared little about their academic progress, social experiences, and general well-being beyond the gridiron. (Phillips, p. 343)

Gaining support from black athletes including his

own teammates proved problematic for LaMarr. BSA President Barry Amis explained, "Michigan State was interesting because it had prominent black students, most of them football players, and many of those football players, the majority, came from the South—Texas, Bubba Smith, Jimmy Raye, etc. They weren't "Michiganders," and

BSA President Barry Amis (right) presenting MSU President Hannah with a list of demands.
Photo courtesy of Michigan State News

they weren't invested in Michigan the way people in Michigan were. They were interested in their athletic careers, and they didn't want to jeopardize those careers. Many of those athletes [including LaMarr] were pro prospects, so they weren't going to do anything that might jeopardize their opportunities. Some of these athletes at other schools not only got thrown off teams but literally got thrown out of school [for protesting]. Many regular students weren't willing to put things on the line either."

Nevertheless, LaMarr was able to assemble a team of MSU athletes from several sports that were sympathetic to his cause:

> During the winter term of 1968, each team for which black athletes competed at Michigan State chose a leader to represent them: basketball – Lee Lafayette, track and field –Don Crawford, soccer – Tony Keyes, and football-LaMarr Thomas. These four student athletes, along with leaders from the Black Student Alliance, met with Dr. Robert Green, Associate Professor of Educational Psychology and an African American, to organize their complaints and demands. (Phillips, pp.349-350)

By the end of March of 1968, they had specified their concerns:

1. The recruitment of black coaches for all sports at the university, such as football, basketball, track, and swimming.

2. The feeling that the Athletic Department tended to discourage black students from participating in certain sports, especially baseball.

3. MSU did not employ black trainers nor a medical doctor to treat all athletes.

4. MSU did not employ black people in Jenison Fieldhouse, the Intramural Building, the ticket office, and Ice Arena, and in non-professional positions.

5. The athletic counselor is under undue pressure in attempting to assist all athletes in academics and should be employed to assist in counseling. This need was highlighted by the fact that many black athletes fail.

6. The academic counseling provided for black athletes was designed to place them in courses that would maintain their eligibility and not enable them to graduate at the end of the four-year period. Athletes are forced to take nonacademic courses such as physical education when they need courses which will make them eligible for graduation.

7. MSU has never elected a black cheerleader. BSA found this questionable in view of the considerable number of talented black girls on the campus.

(Smith, John Matthew. *Black Power in Green and White.* p. 105)

Only two questions remained: When should they present these complaints/demands to the MSU administration, and what should they do if their complaints/demands were not addressed?

A tragic historic event forced the answers.

CHAPTER 16

April 4, 1968, 6:00 p.m.

Dr. King, wearing a dark suit and tie, stepped from Room 306 at the Lorraine Motel in Memphis and gazed over the railing. The temperature was a near-perfect 74 degrees, but ominous dark clouds had formed above. Immediately after his close friend Andrew Young warned him to bring a coat to dinner because of a predicted weather change, a shot rang out. A bullet had entered Dr. King's right cheek and shattered his spinal cord. Dr. Martin Luther King Jr. was pronounced dead at 7:05 p.m. at St. Joseph's Hospital.

The news shocked and grieved Dr. Green beyond words. As Education Director for the Southern Christian Leadership Conference, he, his wife and children had become close to King, Coretta Scott King, and their children. He and Dr. King had met two years earlier at that very motel to plan the March Against Fear from Memphis to Jackson, Mississippi.

The assassination sparked riots and demonstrations across the nation. Pent up anger over segregation and discrimination exploded in Washington D.C, Baltimore, Chicago, and other cities, big and small. Nonviolent mourning demonstrations erupted into full scale riots. Others remained peaceful.

Dr. Green described the reaction at MSU in *At the Crossroads of Fear and Freedom*:

> The evening of King's assassination, about thirty black student activists came to my home to express anger and grief. They wanted to do something, but they didn't know what. Violence was already breaking out in many cities, and I wanted to ensure that the students had an outlet so they would not engage in violence.
>
> I had that in mind when I proposed to these activists that we should hold a campus memorial meeting the following day involving faculty and students. Some of the students said they wanted an all-black meeting, and I insisted that it would be an integrated gathering, in the spirit of Dr. King.
>
> I told them, "I don't care what you think. I care what King would think!"

The next day, 1500 students and faculty members marched peacefully through the campus and held a memorial service. Some held signs that read, "Black is beautiful, so was King," while others sang, "We Shall Overcome."

The following week, tensions calmed, but King's death ignited college activist groups to protest racial discrimination. *Newsweek* sportswriter Dick Schaap's report about a college football team that had started their spring training practices early provided a catalyst for the MSU black athletes to protest. According to Schaap, when athletes approached a white assistant coach about missing practice to participate in events honoring Martin Luther King Jr., the coach responded that the assassination had "nothing to do with practice." Schaap commented that this "typified the insensitivity of many white coaches to the problems faced by African Americans, including their players." The MSU black athletes' question, (When should we present our grievances to the MSU administration?) had been answered—Now.

The plan was simple. Spring football practice had already begun and would continue throughout the summer until the first game in September. LaMarr would lead the charge of black athletes and BSA members and deliver their demands on April 22nd. If the demands were not met, black athletes would boycott all sports, starting with the nationally known Spartan football team, MSU's top moneymaker.

On April 17th, Duffy unknowingly raised the stakes when he announced his starting backfield in an interview with the *Ironwood Daily Globe*:

> Daugherty said that his first picks for the remainder of the backfield [after naming Bill Feraco as his starting quarterback] would be LaMarr Thomas and Frank Waters at halfs and Regis Cavenger at fullback.

Losing LaMarr and other black players such as Charles Bailey and Don Highsmith to a boycott would not sit well with Duffy or the administration.

LaMarr leaving closed conference with "Biggie" Munn
Photo courtesy of Michigan State News

With Dr. Green's approval, LaMarr and two other black athletes took their demands to Athletic Director "Biggie" Munn. According to LaMarr and the others, Munn treated them "with total disrespect." He laughed and crossed out grievances and demands, one-by-one, and declared them "invalid." He said, "Ho, ho, I guess you want a black ticket manager or something." They grabbed the list and stormed out. LaMarr said, "We're going to see President Hannah."

"The boys were angry," Dr. Green said, and the boycott was on.

The next day, they took their grievances to Dr. Hannah, but the MSU President was attending a U.S. Civil Rights Commission. Dr. John Fuzak, Chairman of the Athletic Council and MSU's Big 10 Faculty Representative, and Munn met with them at Holden Hall. LaMarr said, "Munn remained negative and arrogant. He showed a great lack of concern and seemed to take this as a joke."

Munn put on a different face for the press and answered LaMarr's assessment, "Not so. The problem is our concern and the nation's." Privately, when Dr. Green asked him why he had never hired a black assistant coach, Munn answered, "Blacks aren't smart enough to coach."

On April 25th, thirty-eight black athletes boycotted their practice sessions. Twenty-four were football players, including LaMarr, Charles Bailey, and Frank Taylor. They walked off the practice field to attend a grievance meeting. The boycott made national headlines, and every newspaper that covered Big 10 sports reported the story.

Duffy was beside himself.

"What did I do wrong?" he asked Dr. Green.

"You didn't do anything wrong, Duffy," Dr. Green answered. "These youngsters are protesting discrimination in the larger society."

Benjamin Paul Phillips expanded on Dr. Green's answer in his dissertation *All-American Activism*:

> Michigan State responded to local stimuli and
> grievances, but their boycotts were inseparable from
> the greater struggles of black athletes throughout the
> country and of African Americans living in the Civil
> Rights era. Students did not live their lives entirely
> separated from the greater world.
> (Phillips, p. 46)

The strike continued the following day, and LaMarr, as spokesperson, threatened the boycott would extend to include all sports for the rest of the year if the Athletic Department did not respond to their demands. That was enough for Fuzak and Munn. They agreed to the following:

1. A black football coach and black track coach would be hired by September 1.

2. The athletic department would make an active effort at recruiting black swimmers and baseball players.

3. A black athletic counselor would be hired.

4. More black people would be hired as employees for athletic and intramural operations at Michigan State.

5. Michigan State agreed to meet with the protestors again in June to check on the progress of their demands.

LaMarr announced to the Athletic Department and the press that the black athletes had met and agreed to accept the remedies.

The boycott ended, but LaMarr's troubles had just begun.

CHAPTER 17

April 27, 1968, 10:36 a.m.

A long, shrill whistle rang out from Spartan Stadium.

The running play ended, and defensive players emerged from the pile that left LaMarr lying on his back and writhing in pain. Two assistant coaches helped LaMarr stand on one leg and hop off the field. Two firsts: the first inter-squad scrimmage for the 1968 Spartan football team and the first practice after the two-day black athletes' boycott.

Injured spokesman

LaMarr Thomas, unofficial spokesman for MSU's black athletes, is shown being helped off the field after injuring himself in Saturday's inter-squad scrimmage. After not attending football practice Thursday and Friday, the black athlete called off their boycott.

Photo courtesy of Michigan State News

LaMarr sat on a gurney in the training room and held an icepack on his swollen knee. Gayle Robinson, head trainer, diagnosed the injury as a sprained ligament— painful, but not serious. The faint sound of shoulder pads colliding, whistles, and yelling from coaches on the sidelines and students in the stands seeped through the closed door separating the medical training area from the field. LaMarr had to wonder, was this an accident or an act of revenge? After all, he had played and practiced organized football for over six years and had never sustained a serious injury. At the same time, this was a violent sport. "Dancing is a contact sport," Duffy had told the press. "Football is a collision sport." LaMarr knew that some players resented him for leading the boycott—mostly white players, but some black players didn't fully support the strike, either. The nature of football made it easy to disguise a purposeful assault as an innocent part-of-the-game: a missed block, a late hit, an assistant coach waiting too long to whistle a play dead, and many more opportunities to allow a player or players to be injured. Some teammates and spectators suggested this possibility, and others, including his roommate and fellow running back Earl Anderson, refuted the idea, "No, it was an accident. He never got hit."

Although aware of some hard feelings toward him, LaMarr would never accuse teammates of wrongdoing without proof. He was a team player and put on a game face when the press questioned him.

"How did the white players receive you and the other black players when you returned from the boycott?" a *State News* reporter asked.

"I think that we were received very well," LaMarr said, "but it's hard to say. We have only been back one day."

"Were the white players being sympathetic to your actions?"

"Perhaps, but we don't discuss things like this out on the field. We are out there to play."

During that summer of 1968, LaMarr felt the pressure of "serving two masters," the Black Students' Alliance and the MSU Spartan Football Team. The press had labeled him "Spokesman for Black Athletes' Rights." National attention on the boycott meant that he not only served as an activist for MSU black athletes' causes via the BSA, but also as a national advocate. At the same time, as a lifelong "team player," he felt obliged to apply his talents unselfishly for Duffy and his teammates.

His role as an activist challenged him in a new way. For the first time in his life, he received public adversity. Alumni and private citizens sent hate mail to him, other black boycotters, and MSU President Hannah. Alumnus Edward Soergel cancelled his season tickets and referred to LaMarr and other black athletes as "the privileged few," and he could not "support a university or an Administration that doesn't have the guts to stand up to a minority group of any students, let alone one who was not even poor and downtrodden." Another alumnus wrote that many alumni felt that "Negroes have been treated more than fairly in the athletic department, and scholarships to these students have almost outnumbered those to white athletes." In his article "Breaking the Plane," John Matthew Smith wrote, "Black athletes not only took positions away from white players on the field, but also their activism threatened the social order and political power held by whites at the university. To many whites the presence of too many blacks in the athletic program endangered the prestige and good image of their school."

Another challenge involved his obligation to follow up on the demands. LaMarr had supplied the names of seven undergraduate female cheerleading candidates which Dr. Fuzak ignored. LaMarr became upset with the Administration's failure to act on its promise to address the demands:

> "The black athletes are treated like dogs ... The whole
> thing was to take advantage of young black people.
> It is animalistic ... It [the boycott] really did nothing
> to change the program. It really ended up being a
> symbolic protest. I think we messed up when we called

off the boycott after only two days, because … like whities will make promises just to keep blacks quiet for the moment. The brief time of the boycott made it appear as if it was no big deal," he said. (Phillips, p.353)

LaMarr may have underestimated the power of the boycott. Receiving national attention, the MSU boycott may have ignited more protests all over the country. The following universities staged similar strikes and walkouts that summer: Berkley, University of Texas, University of Oklahoma, University of Kansas, Marquette, Washington State University, Howard University, Western Michigan University, and Duffy Daugherty's and "Biggie" Munn's alma mater, Syracuse University.

Serving his other "master," the football team, had never been more difficult for LaMarr. His injured knee was not responding well to the intense therapy provided by the MSU athletic trainers and medical staff. As summer practices wore on, LaMarr's knee injury worsened. The *Traverse City Record Eagle* reported:

LaMarr Thomas at tailback is the closest thing there is to an ace going into drills starting Friday, August 30. But the rangy Markham, Illinois junior who was the team's second leading rusher isn't a shoo-in for his position. He had a bad leg injury and had junior Don Highsmith of New Brunswick, N.J., the team's fastest running back, and sophomore darter Tommy Love of Sylva, N.C. tramping on his heels.

The next day, August 31st, all major newspapers reported this United Press International sports story:

MSU Loses Top Back

EAST LANSING (UPI) — Michigan State's fall football fortunes suffered a heavy blow Friday when it was learned halfback LaMarr Thomas, leading returning rusher for the Spartans, will miss the 1968 campaign because of a knee injury.

Thomas, who gained 211 yards rushing and another 113 on pass receptions last year, is slated to undergo surgery to his right knee to correct a chronic ailment which had him limping as ing as Michigan State opened its fall drills Friday.

"We will do exploratory surgery to find out just what is wrong with the knee," said Dr. James Feurig, team physician. "In any event he will be lost for the year."

Thomas, who was an outstanding back in his high school days in Chicago, hurt the knee last spring and it apparently failed to respond to treatment during the summer.

While the Spartans took the field against Syracuse during the opening game of the 1968 football season, LaMarr, after exploratory surgery, lay in a bed at Sparrow Hospital, two miles west of Spartan Stadium. Dr. Lanny Johnson walked into LaMarr's room to deliver the prognosis.

CHAPTER 18

"It's wrong! You're not supposed to treat people this way."

LaMarr sat on the edge of his hospital bed and cried.

His mother and sister Tina had never seen him so depressed. They were visiting him following his second surgery to repair the torn ligament in his knee. After the first operation, the exploratory surgery, Dr. Johnson had delivered good news, "We can fix your knee, and with some rehabilitation work, you should be good as new for next season. You already knew you'd be out this year, so overall, the prognosis for a full recovery is quite good."

"That's not the way you treat people," he kept repeating, as Tina remembered.

"Exactly what he meant by that, I don't remember," Tina said. "He thought Michigan State didn't treat him and all black athletes well once they got hurt. When my mother and I went to see him, he said he was done with football and MSU."

Perhaps being "sidelined" with a damaged knee gave him time to think about his past two years at MSU—to compare the royal treatment he received as a promising, and later, a productive athlete to the negative treatment he encountered now as an activist and moreover, a wounded player. Victor Jackson, one of LaMarr's closest friends who would eventually become a medical doctor, summed up LaMarr's spirit at that time, "The injury was more to his heart than his knee."

Without LaMarr, the Spartan football team had another less-than-mediocre season. They ended up 2-5 in the Big 10 Conference and 5-5 overall, but LaMarr couldn't have cared less. He felt the Athletic Department had ignored him and other injured athletes during the fall of 1968. Only a select few people knew his intention to quit football and pursue the path of scholar/activist: Dr. Green, his family, Richard and June Thomas, and his roommate, sophomore running back Earl Anderson.

Earl was LaMarr's last link to football. "We were like brothers," Earl said. "I was sort of a quiet, unassuming guy, and LaMarr was outspoken and spoke up for me sometimes. I had family in Wisconsin and Georgia, and on breaks and some holidays, he went with me [for visits]."

During the fall term of 1968, LaMarr nurtured his friendships with students associated with the Black Students' Alliance and Dr. Green. He began a relationship with Claire "Squeaky" McClinton, a co-ed and member of the Black Students' Alliance. He also focused more on his studies and officially declared his major as Social Science. His course load for the 1968-69 year included Introduction to Political Science, Humanities, Negro in Americas, Negro in United States, International Communism, Modern Colonial Africa, Modern American Society, Studies in African History, African Contributions to Society, Independent Studies, and Honors Work.

LaMarr dreaded facing his father during the Christmas/New Year break of 1968-69. Clarence had taken his son's decision to quit football hard. Nevertheless, Clarence and the family loved and supported LaMarr unconditionally.

Upon returning to MSU after the break, he had one more person to face - Duffy Daugherty. Spring practice would start on Monday, March 23rd. It was only fair to inform Duffy of his decision before that time. LaMarr risked losing his scholarship. Moreover, he risked losing Duffy's respect. LaMarr never blamed Duffy for the way he was treated as a black athlete. He blamed society's treatment of blacks. The MSU Administration and Athletic Department merely reflected that treatment. He admired Duffy and valued his leadership.

"We're attacking the system, not the coaches or any of the white athletes," LaMarr explained during the boycott.

Duffy, however, never saw it that way; he took it personally. Later, in his autobiography, he referred to the boycott as the "so-called black problem" and the organization as the "so-called Black Student Alliance."

"There were a couple of coaches that thought LaMarr was arrogant," Dr. Green had said, "but Duffy had a tremendous amount of respect for LaMarr."

On Thursday, March 20, 1969, LaMarr entered Duffy's office. To LaMarr's surprise, Duffy had already known of LaMarr's intention to quit football.

"Michigan State University is like a small town," Duffy explained. "Word gets around."

In the end, they shook hands and Duffy allowed LaMarr to retain his four-year scholarship.

Leaving Duffy's office, LaMarr walked over the Spartan Stadium Football Field for the last time. The sod was still a wintry yellow, but the air was sixty degrees; it was the first day of spring, the season of new life.

PART 3:
BREAKING OUT

CHAPTER 19

April 28, 1969

Exactly one year and a day after the black athlete boycott, LaMarr and 100 black students walked into the Wilson Hall dorm cafeteria and staged a sit-in that shut down its operations. The previous day, three full-time black employees walked off their jobs when Joseph Trantham and Jennie Miller, the food service managers, made racial comments toward them.

LaMarr no longer claimed the title of leading halfback rusher for the MSU Spartan football team. The student body and the MSU administration officially designated him a principal spokesperson for the Black Students' Alliance. Three weeks prior to the sit-in, Acting MSU President Walter Adams convened a committee to find a new MSU president following President Hannah's announcement to retire. The committee consisted of nine faculty members, two undergraduate students, one alumnus, and one black student representative - LaMarr Thomas.

The sit-in gradually precipitated into a major event. Outside the cafeteria, angry white students gathered to protest the protest. Acting President Adams showed up and white students asked, "Wouldn't university police forcibly remove white students who took over the cafeteria?"

Adams replied, ""They [white students] weren't angry. They had not suffered deprivation. They did not belong to an oppressed minority, were not subjected to indignities and discrimination. They really did not have any deep-seated, long-festering grievances against society."

The comment provoked more white students to join those outside the cafeteria, and, in reaction, more black students to participate in the sit-in. Within hours, hundreds of students had gathered inside and outside of Wilson Hall. The media showed up and the incident made national news.

LaMarr and the BSA had a full-scale revolt rising that could easily evolve into a riot. They turned for guidance to Dr. Green, who was now not only an associate professor but also Assistant Director of the Center for Urban Affairs. During the two-day sit-in, LaMarr and Dr. Green worked to resolve the situation.

"LaMarr was a key person in helping me draw up a statement of protest." Dr. Green recalled.

Dr. Green stated to the administration and over 1,000 students gathered at Wilson Hall, "This is the culmination of a series of incidents. I wholeheartedly support the shutdown. The two managers should be fired. I am willing to stake my job and reputation on this demand."

A formal written demand called for the removal of both managers and a commitment to reform racist practices in the workplace. The two managers were fired and the administration signed a commitment to improve working conditions concerning race. Dr. Green cautioned the administration, "In the future—and this is a warning—when racism exists in a component of this institution, we will close that component down."

The success of the protest came with a price. LaMarr and the BSA became targets for slander and the potential physical violence of racists. Many vocal threats and insults toward LaMarr came indirectly through messages to Adams:

> One particularly abusive letter called the protestors "black baboons" and called for them to be mowed down "without mercy – carpet the street with their dead – and the survivors will become the 'good n-----.'" (Phillips, p.372)

LaMarr accepted the racist disdain, but it was new to him. Through his own experience, Dr. Green counseled him that the threats, unfortunately, came with the territory of being an activist for racial justice. Referring to the black athlete boycott that Dr. Green had endorsed the preceding year, he told LaMarr and others, "I received more hate mail than I ever received when I was involved [with Martin Luther King, Jr.] in open housing protests and busing. Community members also called our house at all hours with one caller saying, 'N-----, we gonna run you out of East Lansing yet' with another adding that 'when the faculty becomes more effectively organized, we're gonna run you and all the other blacks off this campus.'" (Phillips, p.393)

Word of LaMarr's status as a national black activist reached home. The unconditional love he received from his family was not shared by all in the Chicagoland area. Sportswriters dismissed him as a disappointment. John E. Meyers editor of the *Chicago Heights Star* and its many subsidiaries wrote: "Thomas turned militant at East Lansing and, because of this, there are some who once admired him much but prefer not to talk about him now. On the other hand, there are some of us who admired Thomas more for the changes he made in himself. This is said without recommending his way as a course of action for everyone. Each man hears his own drummer."

At LaMarr's alma mater, Thornton Township High School, talk about adding a LaMarr Thomas Room in the sports complex ceased. A varsity assistant football coach told players, "Thanks to

LaMarr Thomas, there won't be any Michigan State University scholarships given to Thornton athletes anymore."

By May of 1969, LaMarr had transitioned from star athlete to national activist; however, he did not consider the transition complete. He didn't want to be perceived as "a dumb jock-turned-militant." He wanted recognition as a scholar/athlete. The scholar part had been missing.

That changed on June 5th.

CHAPTER 20

On June 5, 1969, this article appeared on the front page of the *Markham Tribune*:

LaMarr Thomas Elected to MSU Honor Society

La Marr Thomas, son of Mr. and Mrs. Clarence Thomas, Jr., of 1619 West 163rd street, Markham, was among 13 men selected for membership in "Excalibur," senior men's honorary fraternity at Michigan State university.

Each spring, the current members 'tap' 13 juniors to join the 48-year old organization.

At MSU, Excalibur was an honorary society founded in 1921. Each year, seniors were chosen (at the end of their junior year) based on service, leadership, character, and scholarship. They held weekly meetings to discuss their activities and projects.

The key criterion for LaMarr was "scholarship." He had entered Michigan State University as a High School All-American football player. By the end of his sophomore year, he had established himself as a star collegiate running back. The MSU administration and the press recognized him as a national activist for black rights following his leadership during the black athlete boycott and the Wilson Hall sit-in. Becoming an Excalibur member crowned him as a scholar.

He would reenter MSU as an undergraduate senior with the title "scholar/activist."

What LaMarr was NOT was a "militant," as *Chicago Heights Star* editor John E. Meyers and others had labeled him. Dr. Green often defended LaMarr on that point, "LaMarr was not a militant or a nationalist. The militants were intimidated by him. LaMarr protected me from these so-called 'militants.' Example: Some nationalist students said to me, 'We should leave and go to an all-black university,' and LaMarr responded, 'No, let's stay here [at MSU] and make it better.' LaMarr could talk sense to the most radical students."

The protests and his academic studies left LaMarr exhausted by the end of the 1968-69 school year. He cherished going home to family and friends that summer rather than staying on campus for football training as he had in the past.

HK Hall and Victor Jackson were both home in Markham after graduating with honors from their respective universities. HK had set numerous school records while playing for the University of Wyoming and was named Special Mention All American player by several national publications. Victor had been accepted to Meharry Medical College School of Medicine in Nashville, Tennessee and would start post-graduate work in the fall.

That summer, Victor, HK, LaMarr, and Victor's older

brother, Bob, would often discuss politics and social problems—university protests and the Chicago riots were popular topics. One question they explored was "Why were blacks in big cities burning their own neighborhoods?" They concluded that urban blacks living in inner cities were not property owners like their families in Markham. They vented their frustrations and had little or nothing to lose by destroying their surroundings.

For the first time in six years, LaMarr started a fall school term as a student and not a "student athlete." He nurtured his reputation as a scholar/activist by focusing on his academic studies and participating in social protests and demonstrations. With the goals of achieving a Bachelor of Arts degree at the end of the spring term and expanding his cultural views, he registered for challenging courses such as African Language-Elementary Swahili, Cultural Personality, American Political Thought, Traditional Oriental Thought, and Sociological Theory.

He also kept active in the Black Students' Alliance; however, diverse points of view within the BSA membership led to internal conflicts and more black activist organizations forming on campus. One group, the Black Liberation Front (BLF), emerged amidst controversy. The roots of the BLF were in Great Britain with the goal of globally linking black struggles. The BSA leadership (LaMarr, Richard Thomas, Jason LaVette, Barry Amis, and Ron Bailey) were not consulted about the formation of the BLF at MSU and viewed its emergence as a coup since it siphoned a portion of the BSA membership.

The public perception of the Black Liberation Front was militancy which contradicted the philosophy of peaceful resistance, the viewpoint of Martin Luther King, Jr., Dr. Green, and the BSA. Specifically, many people associated the Black Liberation Front with the Black Liberation Army and the Black Panthers with violent tactics.

Richard Thomas said, "At that time, I wasn't interested in contesting it and causing a lot of conflict but was warned about getting caught up in that stuff."

Kamithi Mohammed, student activist and author of books on the Black Power movement in Michigan, was asked to serve on the BLF Executive Board. He responded, "In the interest of reaching some type of political stability among African students who are searching for better ways of pressuring the establishment here at Michigan State University, I will not accept a position on the executive council of the Black Liberation Front."

LaMarr realized that the BLF was not going away. Rather than ignore it and let it fester into a radical group at MSU, he chose to join the BLF and change it from within. Even though he wanted to keep a low profile to not be identified as a member, his leadership qualities couldn't be ignored and the BLF held an election and issued the following statement in *The Westside News* on May 16, 1970:

> The members of the new executive board are George Fleming, Tony Martin, LaMarr Thomas, Bill Powers, and Stan McClinton... It should be noted that the peoples' newly elected organization continues support of the Office of Black Affairs [created in conjunction with the BSA and later renamed Office of Multicultural Affairs] and will continue to promote a harmonious relationship.

The statement gave fodder to LaMarr's critics who used it as evidence that LaMarr Thomas was "a dangerous black militant."

LaMarr did not participate in any of the BLF's activities. Racial protests on college campuses diminished to a degree and gave way to anti-Viet Nam War demonstrations across the country. During an anti-war demonstration on May 4, 1970, U.S. National Guardsmen shot and killed four students at Kent

State University, only 250 miles from MSU. One of the slain students, Jeffrey Miller, had transferred from MSU to Kent State just four months earlier. It resulted in four million students going on strike among 450 universities and colleges, including at Michigan State.

By the end of May, the protesting had calmed, but many universities had closed early, and graduation ceremonies were cancelled. MSU stayed open, and LaMarr graduated with honors on June 14, 1970.

CHAPTER 21

Sunday, June 14, 1970, late afternoon

It was 80 degrees and cloudy when LaMarr stood in Spartan Stadium. Instead of wearing a football uniform, he wore a cap and gown. His mother, father, sister, and brother had just left for the long trip home to Markham, Illinois. Fewer and fewer small groups of family members snapping pictures of their graduate dotted the field.

Now what? This, the question all graduates must ask themselves at some point, had reached a deadline for an answer. LaMarr, methodical and analytical, had worked out his plan. In the short-term, he would pick up his official diploma on Monday at Hannah Administrative Building. Next, he would close out his housing and any utility matters. Most importantly, he would apply to the Michigan State University Graduate School of Arts & Letters as a history major.

His long-term goal was to further his education and nurture his dream of being a scholar/activist. This vision presented challenges; the leading one being money. His undergraduate scholarship had expired. During the previous four years, he was able to supplement his income by tutoring, writing, and conducting research for other students and professors. That wouldn't cover the cost of graduate classes, books, and housing, but he had all summer to address his financial problems.

He needed a long-deserved vacation. HK had invited him to Denver where the Denver Nuggets (at that time, called the Denver Rockets) had drafted him to play professional basketball. HK's stellar seasons playing for the University of Wyoming had earned him offers from the Nuggets, the Chicago Bulls, and even the Dallas Cowboys football team.

LaMarr flew to Denver and the two buddies spent the week together. After HK's training sessions, they drove to Wyoming where HK settled housing issues at the university, and the two drove back to Chicago together.

"It was a good bonding experience," HK recalled. "We talked about many things—politics and such. After that, we might not see each other for a year or more, but we'd always keep in touch. We were always close. I always knew where he was, what he was doing, where he was working, how he and Chris were coming along."

LaMarr and Chris maintained a "long-distance" relationship. For the prior several years, they had communicated via letters and phone calls and had agreed to date other people. His relationship with Claire "Squeaky" McClinton and the BSA had ended when he graduated.

Living at home in Markham that summer, LaMarr accepted the pluses and minuses of becoming a scholar/activist. On the positive side, it was a life of learning. Since his early years at Warren Palm Elementary, he loved reading, researching, writing, and discussing. His mentor, Dr. Green, taught, served as a college administrator, published, and fought for causes he believed in. LaMarr craved that life. The negative side would always be money. Others would think him crazy for throwing away the possibility of a lucrative career as a pro athlete for the meager earnings of a teacher or researcher, but LaMarr didn't care; in the long run, he would be living his dream.

LaMarr would have to work at any job that paid for books and classes before achieving a master's degree and perhaps, a doctoral degree leading to a position as an instructor, researcher, or professional advocate for causes. He worked a construction job that summer, and it paid well. From that moment on, he would take on any job that would support his addiction to scholarly learning. Whether it was dishwashing or disc jockeying, he would view the position as an adventure, an experience to support his life of learning.

By the end of summer, LaMarr had earned enough money to pay for tuition and room and board for one year of graduate school at MSU. During the 60s and 70s, a college education was inexpensive. If he doubled his course load and earned extra cash tutoring, writing, and researching for others, LaMarr could finish a two-year program in one year. Always the "team player," he convinced himself that he wasn't doing it for selfish reasons. He was working hard to become an intelligent social activist for a better society, the largest and most important "team" he had ever felt a part of.

His close friend and activist colleague from the BSA, Richard Thomas, registered for the same graduate program. LaMarr, Richard, and Richard's fiancé, June, were not partyers.

LaMarr and Richard
Photo courtesy of Richard and June Thomas

They often closed the library on Saturday nights. Richard, a serious student and black activist, was also a highly respected poet in the literary world. His poetry had appeared in anthology publications including *A Galaxy of Black Writing*,

Black Fire, and *Negro Digest.*

There was a price to pay for their close association. Along with others involved in racial boycotts and protests in the name of the Black Students' Alliance and/or the Black Liberation Front, the FBI tracked LaMarr and Richard with surveillance. COINTELPRO, the FBI's counterintelligence program of the 1960s and '70s, spied on a wide range of individuals, including black activist leaders. The program justified warrantless wiretapping if, as the FBI policy stated, "...it is necessary to protect the United States against a clear or present danger to the structure or the existence of its government."

LaMarr rented an apartment off-campus in September of 1970 before starting his post-graduate studies. About a week into his stay, someone knocked on his door. A man dressed in a Michigan Bell Telephone Service uniform said, "I need to do some minor repairs on your phone. There's been a problem since the installation." LaMarr allowed him inside to do the purported work. It didn't seem unusual since he recently had the telephone service as well as other utilities installed and established in his name, but when he mentioned this to Richard and others, they became concerned.

"We always suspected that someone was following us or tapping our phones," Richard said. "We'd even take them apart to see if we could find anything in them."

Their untrained eyes for technical surveillance devices didn't detect anything. Nevertheless, for the next several years, whenever LaMarr moved into a new residence, the same telephone-serviceman-experience followed him.

On September 3, 1971, LaMarr earned a Master of Arts degree in history. Most graduate programs at MSU required a two-year commitment of course completion plus passing a comprehensive test or a thesis approval. LaMarr and Richard completed the requirements within one year.

Richard and June married and moved to Ann Arbor, Michigan where they took courses at the University of Michigan and applied to Michigan's doctoral program. LaMarr followed them to Ann Arbor and enrolled in courses. After two semesters at U of M, teaching part-time at a junior college, and working at odd jobs, LaMarr questioned himself: Do I want to apply to a doctoral program at U of M? Should I return to MSU and work for Dr. Green and toward a doctorate degree? Maybe I should return to Chicago and work for a while until I can decide on my future…

He studied the paths of the people close to him. Richard and June were not only pursuing PhDs but also starting a family with the birth of a baby daughter. Dr. Green was moving up the academic ladder at MSU. Now a full professor and Director of the Center for Urban Affairs, the administration would soon name him the Dean of the College of Urban Development. Harry Oryhon, his friend since childhood, had graduated from the University of Illinois and entered a school of dentistry. NBA and ABA basketball teams kept pursuing HK, but he had been considering entering the business world. Victor Jackson had completed graduate school and started medical school in Nashville. LaMarr's sister Tina and her son had also moved to Nashville. It was a university town and he would be close to family and a close friend.

He picked up the receiver of his FBI-wiretapped phone and made a call.

CHAPTER 22

Spring, 1972

LaMarr drove west on Jefferson Street just north of downtown Nashville, Tennessee. He turned south onto 21st Avenue and entered the campus of Meharry Medical College. Victor lived in an apartment complex on campus, and LaMarr pulled into the parking lot adjacent to it.

After the seven-hour trip from Ann Arbor, Michigan, he sighed and smiled. Vanderbilt University sat a mile and a half south, and Tennessee State University was less than a mile west of Meharry Medical College. Nashville hosted the campuses of sixteen more colleges and universities, and each featured a bookstore stocked with history, philosophy, and various political and social science books. Factoring in the thousands of students and professors, LaMarr had landed in a scholar's paradise.

Victor helped LaMarr move into the two-bedroom apartment with him. When LaMarr had finally settled in, he said, "Victor, I need to tell you something. The phone company is going to come and say, 'we need to do some work on your phone' within a week."

"What's that about?"

"Victor, the FBI is tracking me wherever I go."

Within a week, an individual wearing a South-Central

Bell Telephone uniform serviced the phone. "We'd look out the window and a cop car was sitting outside," Victor said. "He [LaMarr] was looked upon as a radical, and he was anything but—he was a peacemaker."

For the next eighteen months, the two men lived in harmony. Victor needed solitude and peace so he could study when not attending his medical classes and seminars. At the same time, he needed companionship and social relief from the grueling life of a medical student. LaMarr understood that and respected Victor's space. He created his own life visiting college campuses and bookstores, reading, attending lectures, and even leading discussion groups on campuses and at the apartment.

"He read and studied constantly," Victor said. "I thought, 'Damn, here I am at medical school, and he's working as hard as I am.' He'd meet with students, and they'd just sit and talk. It was amazing. He attracted people. His big presence and soft voice of wisdom. He was a mentor."

Victor noticed that LaMarr had developed a trend when people asked about his past. He played down his football valor at Michigan State because society had a tough time accepting that he had chosen the modest returns of a scholar/activist's life over that of a pro football player. They wanted to believe that his knee injury was a career-ending tragedy. LaMarr's honest nature would not allow him to lie, but he did little to correct the myth. It was easier for them to believe the fiction than to understand the truth.

In Chicago, LaMarr's name appeared on the sports pages again while sportswriters perpetuated the myth. In 1972, a talented athlete's name, Quinn Buckner, dominated the Chicago sports pages. Buckner was a two-sport competitor from the same high school district as LaMarr. The sportswriters couldn't resist comparing/contrasting the careers of the two athletes from

Thornton Township High School District 205. Both African American players led their football and basketball teams to state championships, and both were named to all-state teams. The falsehoods about LaMarr emerged when the reporters contrasted their college careers as John Meyers wrote in *The Star Tribune*, December 28, 1972.

> Buckner seems to have it on Thomas because of what
> he has already achieved in college, at the University of
> Indiana. Thomas did not try for two sports at Michigan
> State, opting for football, and he suffered a knee injury
> which required surgery and ended him as a gridder ...
> Thomas turned militant at East Lansing ...

Enjoying his idyllic life in Nashville, LaMarr cared little about what was said about him back home, but his scholar's paradise came to an end. After a year and a half, Victor left for Louisiana to do his medical residency, and LaMarr had to move out. He, Tina, and his nephew moved to Birmingham, Alabama where they had family nearby and eventually settled in Bethlehem, Alabama, about 100 miles south of their relatives. LaMarr continued his lifestyle of reading and researching. He supported himself by washing dishes in a restaurant. "Those were good times," Tina recalled.

But LaMarr felt something was missing from his life. Outside of family, he always had a girlfriend and girlfriends in his life. Wanda Brown, a friend from MSU, said, "I think LaMarr was a feminist. LaMarr was a great friend to women. He did something that I've never seen another man do, and that is be critical of another man for his treatment of women. Women could go to LaMarr and talk to him about experiencing sex discrimination, and LaMarr would not just lament with her, he would say, "What?" and he would go to that brother or whoever that person was, and he would tell them principally why that was wrong. That was very important for people to see."

Because LaMarr was passionate his love affairs often suffered. He would channel his passions in too many different directions and fail to invest in the relationship. He approached sports, friendships, causes, and academics with a fervor that bordered on obsession. At the same time, he wanted and needed a stable relationship with a woman. He knew only one woman who had always loved and accepted him, his passions, and his chosen way of life. He would often refer to her as "the love of my life," Chris LaVette.

He packed his bags.

CHAPTER 23

June 1973

LaMarr, Tina, and her son arrived in Markham to the joy of Frances, Clarence, and Everett; the family was reunited. As soon as LaMarr had unpacked the car, he dashed into the house and called Christine LaVette.

Chris lived with her parents in Riverdale, only six miles from Markham. She had moved on with her life: commuting to her bank job in downtown Chicago, taking classes at Roosevelt University, and studying ballet. Most significantly, she had a steady boyfriend.

LaMarr asked if he could visit her that afternoon. This put Chris in an awkward position because her boyfriend was due to come over and they had planned to spend the day together. She told LaMarr he could come over then called her boyfriend to tell him of LaMarr's visit. The boyfriend decided to stay away—a mistake because Chris and LaMarr reconnected and rekindled their relationship.

After a summer of dating, they moved into an apartment together in Harvey. Although Chris's mother and stepfather loved LaMarr, her mom did not approve of the living situation. Chris discussed this with LaMarr. She said it would make her mother feel better if they were married, but if LaMarr didn't want to, she was okay with that. Whether it was him or her who proposed didn't matter. LaMarr agreed, and the couple made plans to wed in October of the next year.

On October 12, 1974, LaMarr and Chris wed at the First Federated Church in Harvey, Illinois. Chris's biological father, who lived in Wisconsin, refused to attend the wedding. This upset Chris but not enough to disrupt the joyous occasion. Weeks later, they visited her father and his wife in Wisconsin, and LaMarr, by just being himself, won her dad's approval.

LaMarr longed for the scholarly life he had enjoyed in Nashville, and the opportunity reopened to him. In 1975, Dr. Green returned to MSU from a trip to South Africa where he had studied apartheid. While writing about his experiences on the trip, he resumed his duties as professor, dean, and the NAACP's court expert on school desegregation. In short, he needed scholarly help, and LaMarr was always eager to collaborate with him.

LaMarr applied to the MSU Doctoral College of Arts and Letters as a history major. In the spring of 1975, he received his acceptance letter, and the couple moved into married student housing on campus in East Lansing. Again, LaMarr was living his dream, surrounded by scholarly people, books, lectures, seminars, and a chance to work with his mentor, Dr. Green. Chris, too, enjoyed college life. When they moved onto the MSU campus, she studied at nearby Lansing Community College.

It had been almost a decade since LaMarr had shunned the limelight as a star athlete, but the sports world refused to allow the public to forget him. In December of 1975, the Illinois Basketball Coaches' Association (IBCA) notified LaMarr that he had been elected to the IBCA Hall of Fame and asked him to accept the award at a banquet in March. After the ceremony, Chicago television, radio, and newspaper reporters surrounded him and shouted questions. A *Chicago Daily News* sportswriter asked, "A lot of people out there say you went bad and were crazy for throwing away a pro football career for the life of an activist and a scholar. How do you respond?"

"People said that they never dreamed I'd go bad, but I never went bad. I just got involved. I became more aware of what the real world was all about," LaMarr answered. "In high school, the world is so isolated. I wanted to see what was happening."

Lloyd Batts, who the press called "the second LaMarr Thomas," was inducted into the IBCA Hall of Fame also. As a result, both men were asked to play in a benefit all-star basketball game the next month in Thornton High School's gymnasium against a team of Chicago professional athletes including Chicago Bears quarterback Bobby Douglas.

Press conference after the IBCA Hall of Fame induction, "...I never went bad."
Photo courtesy of the Illinois Basketball Coaches' Association

Batts had starred on the University of Cincinnati's basketball team and later played in both the NBA and the ABA. When they announced Batts' name, the crowd cheered. LaMarr received a mixed reaction. Many cheered, but some booed or remained silent. The response must have hurt LaMarr after receiving many standing ovations in his alma mater's gym during his high school days, but he never showed it.

That same year, another two-sport high school superstar, Herb Simpson, emerged at Thornton high school, and reporters couldn't resist bringing up LaMarr's name again:

"Herb Simpson is probably as fine an all-around athlete as we've had at Thornton since LaMarr

Thomas," claims basketball coach Tom Hanrahan, who is now enjoying Simpson's talents.

In the spring of 1976, LaMarr completed his language (French) requirement for his doctoral program. He and Chris were ready to come home to the Chicago area. They rented an apartment in the far south suburb of Steger, Illinois, close to Governors State University where Chris took classes and worked as an assistant in the Sociology Department. A commuter train ran directly from the university to downtown Chicago where LaMarr found a job with the U.S. Equal Employment Opportunity Commission - Chicago District (EEOC) as a case investigator.

Eventually, the couple bought a house in nearby Park Forest, another south suburb but closer to Chicago and their families.

"We partied a lot back then at my house and Everett's," Tina recalled. "LaMarr did Al Green imitations."

Overall, the Thomas families enjoyed their lives, until tragedy struck.

CHAPTER 24

February 5, 1978, 10:35 a.m.

Clarence Thomas traveled south on Dixie Highway toward the 159th street intersection in Harvey, Illinois, only one mile from his home in Markham. As he proceeded through the intersection, a car heading west on 159th street broadsided his Cadillac on the driver's side door.

Rookie Harvey Police Officer Denard Eaves was summoned to the scene and reported, "His [LaMarr's] father was involved in a 10-50, an auto accident. He was dead at the scene."

LaMarr asked Officer Eaves one question, "Did my father say anything before he died?"

Officer Eaves answered, "No, I'm sorry."

It's difficult to understand what LaMarr may have wanted to hear from his father: I'm sorry? I love you? I'm proud of you? LaMarr often hid his feelings, but those who knew him best offered a theory. LaMarr dealt with his emotions by helping others deal with their feelings. He was the rock in the family, the shoulder for others to cry on during the funeral arrangements and grieving process.

Clarence's death affected LaMarr deeply. As with most father and son relationships, they had their conflicts. Applying strict discipline, Clarence pushed LaMarr hard to succeed throughout

LaMarr's childhood. He never fully accepted LaMarr's decision to reject pro football and enter a life of academic freedom and activism. His unexpected death left this conflict unresolved. Moreover, this was the second time LaMarr had suffered the unforeseen death of someone close due to a car accident—the first being Richie Halbert's passing. If LaMarr experienced the stages of grief (denial, anger, bargaining, depression, and acceptance, according to Elisabeth Kübler-Ross in her book *On Death and Dying*), he experienced them privately. As his sister often reminded, "LaMarr was a private person."

Following his father's death, LaMarr seemed to sink into a depression. "I'm in the valley," he would say whenever he felt down, and it was more than the typical sadness one feels after the loss of a loved one. He was unhappy working at the Equal Employment Opportunity Commission (EEOC).

At first, he was excited about his position. It appeared the perfect job opportunity for an activist. The EEOC is responsible for enforcing federal laws that make it illegal to discriminate against a job applicant or an employee because of the person's race, color, religion, sex (including pregnancy, transgender status, and sexual orientation), national origin, age (40 or older), disability or genetic information. Hired as an investigator, he managed inquiries and complaints of employment discrimination under the Federal statutes enforced by the EEOC. His duties included listening to complaints and gathering evidence that supported or refuted the charges. Lawyers would analyze LaMarr's findings and decide if a violation had occurred. If so, more attorneys would either litigate, mediate, or file a charge.

At his job, LaMarr used his scholarly skill, researching, but as an activist, he was left out of the process. *The Britannica Dictionary* defines an activist as "a person who uses or supports strong actions (such as public protests) to help make changes in politics or society." At the EEOC, the lawyers handled the "actions to help make changes," and most often, because of legality or bureaucracy, the changes were slow, minimal, or nonexistent. All day, LaMarr heard stories of woe and suffering from employees at their workplaces, and at night, he brought his work home either in the form of paperwork or empathy for the employees.

In 1980, a career opportunity for Chris offered a chance to move to Ohio, and the couple took it. Chris had experience and expertise in finance which led to positions in banks and eventually a career as a financial adviser. The move allowed LaMarr to leave his EEOC position and renew his life as a scholar. He took any odd job in the Akron area that permitted him to study at Kent State University, only eleven miles away. In short, LaMarr enjoyed the scholar's life that he relished when he and Victor had lived together in Nashville.

At the same time, Dr. Green's national reputation as an expert on urban education brought him to nearby Cleveland as a consultant for the city's failing school system. LaMarr again helped him with research and writing. Dr. Green recalled those years, "Several school systems who knew of my work and writing, especially with disadvantaged students, offered me work. I had more work than I could ever imagine. LaMarr Thomas was one of those individuals who helped me with background, research and writing, and I made sure he got paid for it."

Dr. Green's career directly influenced LaMarr's life. From 1983 until 1985, Dr. Green served as President of the University of the District of Columbia. Although his duties as the head of a major university occupied most of his time, he never lost his passion for fighting for just causes and authoring scholarly papers. Consequently, LaMarr and other scholars who shared his passions worked even harder fighting, researching, and writing for him.

Within the first year of his tenure at UDC, Dr. Green participated in a sit-in at the South African Embassy, protesting the South African government's treatment of blacks. LaMarr joined in the protest. In 1984, with LaMarr and others' help, Dr. Green wrote "Expectations: A Driving Force in Human Behavior," a research paper that established him as an expert and consultant for public education systems nationwide.

Dr. Green returned to Michigan State University in 1986 as a professor and administrator. Over the next several years, LaMarr continued researching and writing for him. During that time, Dr. Green published one of the most groundbreaking research papers of his career to date: "The Progressive Role of Athletics in American Society: Past, Present, and Future." LaMarr did so much of the research and writing of this paper that Dr. Green felt compelled to offer this dedication on the title page:

> The author wishes to express appreciation to LaMarr
> Thomas, MA., Research Associate at the Center for
> Applied Research, for the research, writing, and
> preparation of this paper.

The paper was officially published in April of 1991, and while LaMarr's academic/activist life flourished, his personal life faltered.

On May 31, 1991, Chris and LaMarr divorced.

CHAPTER 25

LaMarr and Chris kept their reason(s) for divorce private. One might speculate money and job-related problems provided tensions as they often do in marriages. Chris had a steady position and income at a National City Bank in the Akron, Ohio area. LaMarr worked at odd jobs and spent many hours conducting scholarly research for himself and others for little pay, but Chris made it clear that it was not a hostile separation. "It was an amicable, no-fault divorce."

LaMarr moved into an apartment in Copley, Ohio, about nine miles from Akron. He continued attending Kent State University and later moved to Beachwood, Ohio, a suburb of Cleveland. Dr. Green had been doing consulting work for the Cleveland school system through Cuyahoga Community College where LaMarr taught a class and helped Dr. Green with his work.

As Dr. Green's work increased, LaMarr's work escalated, also. The W.K. Kellogg Foundation hired scholars, including Dr. Green, to study and publish works about discrimination in education and other aspects of life. While LaMarr, Dr. Green, and other scholars immersed themselves in projects for the foundation, riots broke out in Los Angeles over the not guilty verdicts of police in the beating of Rodney King, an African American arrested for driving while intoxicated. George White, a former mentee of Dr. Green at MSU, covered the riots for the *Los Angeles Times* and won a Pulitzer Prize for his coverage of them. George White provided the link that allowed Dr. Green and LaMarr to study the dynamics of the uprisings and participate in demonstrations in the Midwest protesting the verdicts.

During LaMarr's busy life as a scholar and activist, tragic news came from home. His mother, Frances Thomas, had died from lung cancer in 1994.

"LaMarr was devastated," Tina recalled. "He loved his momma."

LaMarr returned to Markham and grieved in his own private way. That is, he tried to be the rock in the family by putting his own feelings aside and consoling everyone else, but his mother's death was too much for him. Additionally stressful was the fact that he kept his divorce with Chris a secret from the family. "It had been at least a year or more before I knew anything about the divorce," Tina later said.

After the funeral and before returning to Ohio, LaMarr announced, "I'm in the valley," his signature declaration of feeling depressed. He continued his work as a scholar and an activist, but his heart wasn't in it. Something was missing in his life, and he needed a change. One day in 1998, LaMarr showed up on Chris's doorstep in Akron and said, "I'm going back to Chicago. It's not working out for me here. Do you want to go with me?"

"Yes, I do," Chris answered, and just like that, they reunited.

One of Chris's colleagues at National City Bank suggested they consider moving to the western suburb of Naperville. They rented an apartment in nearby Downers Grove and searched for property in Naperville. Within a year, they settled into a condominium in a quiet Naperville neighborhood, four miles from its downtown area. Chris quickly found a position as a financial adviser, and LaMarr rejoined the EEOC as an investigator. Having worked at that position a decade earlier, he knew the pros and cons of the job. He would be helping people fight discrimination at their workplace, but at the same time, his empathy for the victims' frustrations over their employment situations and government bureaucracy would bring him down. A fellow EEOC investigator summarized the frustration that LaMarr felt this way, "Our souls felt soiled from listening to the dirt employers flung at our claimants, but our hands never seemed to get dirty enough to help them."

To counter the exasperation he felt from his EEOC job, he tapped into his playful side. LaMarr always had a gift for singing and performing. As a side job, he billed himself as *L.T. the D.J. Distinctive Jammin',* and provided entertainment for weddings and parties. He also joined a dancing-singing-lip-syncing group that performed regularly at a suburban nightclub called *The Sabre Room.* In its "heyday," the mid-to-late 70s, Frank Sinatra, Dean Martin, Liberace, Bob Hope, Sammy Davis Jr., and other iconic stars performed there. By the late 90s, *The Sabre Room* mostly hosted banquets and party events, but the nightclub retained its luxurious interior and mystique.

Clarence Hayse, the leader of the dancing-singing-lip-syncing group, recalled those days, "We had

all kinds of names when we'd sing because we'd do the Dells, the Four Tops, the Temps and more. We'd practice at the American Legion Hall down the street in Markham. We would come up with steps and stuff, and LaMarr would always agree with me. LaMarr was in it a couple of years, and then his brother [Everett] took over. We'd sing or lip-sync and do the dance steps. We agreed that we were getting kind of old to be doing all the fancy dance steps, so I think that's why he [LaMarr] dropped out."

Old friendships provided another outlet for LaMarr. Ray Jakubiak, his co-captain on the Thornton High School football team, and Frank Bauman, his former high school football coach, both lived in the Naperville area. Ray was a pilot, and he would occasionally arrange for LaMarr, Frank, and other mutual friends to meet for breakfast at *Charlie's*, a little family restaurant at Clow Airport in nearby Bolingbrook, Illinois where Ray housed his private plane.

Reminiscing with old friends, reading, studying, and occasionally performing kept LaMarr content, but he was never fully pleased with himself if he wasn't helping people and/or fighting for a worthy cause.

On a Saturday morning in 2002, Ray had arranged a get-together breakfast at *Charlie's* for several high school alumni and their spouses. Frank Bauman had been suffering from dementia, and Ray and the others wanted to discuss ways of helping him and his wife cope. Another issue emerged, and it would dynamically change LaMarr's life.

PART 4: TALF

CHAPTER 26

Saturday morning, May 4, 2002

"Thornridge is going bankrupt, and Thornton may be, too."

When Pat Mize, Thornton Township High School special education teacher, made that announcement, the small gathering of Thornton alumni friends at *Charlie's* stopped eating their breakfasts. The shocked group members included LaMarr and Chris, Ray and Wrenne Jakubiak, Harry and Yvonne Oryhon, and Dale Mize, Pat's husband. Having attended Thornton in the 1960s when students enjoyed the fruits of attending a high school supported by one of the richest tax bases in Illinois, their shock was justified.

Dale Mize, the youngest alumnus, had graduated from TTHS as a football star in 1970 and later played defensive tackle at Northwestern University and pro football in the WFL. His love and devotion to his alma mater brought him back to Thornton where he worked in the Special Education Department and coached football. Dale educated the other alumni on the details that led to the high school's financial woes.

In short, all the industry that had bolstered the tax base and made Harvey, Illinois a booming blue-collar suburb had vanished. Cheryl Corley, a Chicago-based NPR correspondent and former resident of Harvey, described a revisit to her hometown:

A drive through Harvey's downtown today is in stark contrast to the bustle of years ago. There are a few banks, a thriving hospital, and a YMCA, but they are vastly outnumbered by vacant and boarded up businesses. The factories closed and other businesses left town; it's been a long fall for Harvey. Today, the village is struggling to survive.

On the street where I lived, about a mile from Thornton High School, the home with the big yard that my parents were so proud of is abandoned and a tattered wreck. The sky is visible through the roof. The awnings my mother added to the structure are faded and frail. The tree I planted in the back yard is towering and strong, but the fence that surrounded the property is gone and boards cover some of the windows. There are more than 1000 vacant and abandoned properties.

Harvey's main street 1966   *Harvey's main street 2002*
Photos courtesy of The Illinois Policy Institute

The poverty-stricken taxpayers rejected a 70% increase in the districts educational tax rate to make up for the $9 million operating deficit and some $60 million in total debt. Closing the over 100-year-old Thornton Township High School became a near-future reality. In the meantime, over 2,000 TTHS students would experience cutbacks in educational programs, extracurricular activities, facilities, and staff. The school couldn't even afford to provide a yearbook.

Recalling the somber mood after the breakfast, Dale commented, "Walking out, LaMarr was in a daze."

"LaMarr, everything cool?" Dale asked him.

"Yeah, thanks for letting us know about the high school," LaMarr answered and appeared deep in thought.

CHAPTER 27

2003

Jane Halegiere Martin was telling a story about her former mentor at Indiana University who had started a scholarship fund for his small, rural alma mater high school. LaMarr listened as if each word brought him closer to a catharsis or an epiphany. He and Chris had been visiting the Martins who lived in Bloomington, Indiana. Jane, Chris, and LaMarr had been friends since their high school days at Thornton. Chris and Jane had been TTHS cheerleaders. Lorna Propes, their former cheerleading coach and a Thornton alumnus, was also visiting the Martins.

After Jane finished her story, LaMarr, sitting across the dinner table from her, suggested, "You know, Thornton is in terrible financial trouble. Maybe we could do something for Thornton like your friend did for his high school." The seed for the Thornton Alumni Legacy Fund was planted and couldn't have been sown into a more fertile garden.

Jane had over thirty years of experience in public and private equity investing. Before working for Village Ventures, Inc., a Massachusetts-based network of Venture Capital Funds, Jane was the Acting Chief Executive Officer at Wisdom Tools, Inc., where she organized the business, recruited the management, raised venture capital from Chicago and Cincinnati, and served as CEO for its first year of operation. By 2002, she had retired from business, but her skills and spirit remained sharp and ready for a challenge.

Chicago Magazine had recently named Lorna Propes among its "30 Toughest Lawyers in Chicago." Decades earlier, she had left a career as a teacher and a coach at TTHS to enter the law profession. She defended and prosecuted individuals and major companies in over 100 jury trials. One of her more infamous cases involved Terry "Tank" Johnson, the former Chicago Bears defensive lineman who had some brushes with the law. Her law partner, Elizabeth A. Kaveny, said of her, "Lorna is like a tornado. You can feel Lorna's energy before she even enters the room, whether it's the office or a courtroom. Then, she is very gregarious, enthusiastic, and aggressive. Everything just gets fast and furious. And then she is gone, just like a tornado." Lorna would later become the Honorable Lorna E. Propes, Circuit Court Judge of Cook County.

LaMarr had been an activist looking for a cause to champion, and Chris supported him and the Thornton cause. LaMarr, Chris, Jane, and Lorna shared a love and loyalty to Thornton High School.

"We came to the agreement that we should start something for TTHS," Jane said.

Ray Jakubiak remembered getting a phone call from either LaMarr or Jane who said, "We need to start contacting Thornton alumni and arrange a meeting at Thornton."

"Out of that, we started getting people together," Ray said. "The meeting was held in the Girls' Club Room or someplace like that at Thornton. Thirty or forty people showed up—Harry Hall, Harry Oryhon, and people from all over. Jane kind of led things."

As the meeting progressed, the leadership dynamics of TALF unfolded. At first, the participants looked toward LaMarr and Ray for leadership. After all, they were remembered as co-captains of a championship Thornton football team, but this wasn't a football game. It was the evolution of a non-profit business, and Jane had earned the reputation of a highly successful businessperson.

"On the football team," Ray recalled, "LaMarr led by example, and that's the role he took on TALF."

During those early monthly meetings, Jane would travel from Bloomington, Indiana to Chicago, and the group established TALF's goals and activities:

- Through Lorna's legal assistance, Thornton Alumni Legacy Fund would be registered as a 501(c)(3) Corporation.

- Mission: Provide for college scholarships and educational and extracurricular opportunities for students attending Thornton Township High School.

- Guiding Quote: "Everywhere we look, caring hands have preceded us." —G.B. Shaw.

- Specific Financial Goal(s): Raise one million dollars, bring back Wildcat Pride, and give TTHS students the opportunity to experience the rich educational programs the alumni had enjoyed.

- Proposed Activities and Methods of Fundraising: Soliciting and accepting alumni donations; Golf outings; Benefit entertainment events; Speaker series; an Alumni and teacher Hall of Fame program; Ideas for activities and fundraising remained open as per approval of the Board of Directors.

The original Board of Directors and list of Charter Members included LaMarr and Chris, and LaMarr took his role seriously. He wanted to be active in every facet of TALF. One of LaMarr's most notable traits was that he was a "people person." One of the most common remarks people would say after meeting him was, "He talked to me like I was the only person on earth, and everything I had to say was important."

Jane's many business skills included recognizing the talents of others and empowering them in activities respective to those talents which made TALF a successful non-profit organization. She recognized LaMarr's "people person" talent and called upon him whenever person-to-person communication was needed. He played a significant role in developing a motivational speaker series for Thornton and assisting in choosing Hall of Fame nominees.

"Pamela Barnes [a TTHS alumnus and future TALF President] and LaMarr worked on getting speakers," Ray Jakubiak recalled. "She and LaMarr would literally go up in the Thornton library and go through the yearbooks and say, 'Who would be good to talk to?'"

LaMarr convinced over twenty Thornton alumni to come to the high school and speak to the students about their successful careers. One of the earliest speakers was comedian/actor/writer Tom Dreesen who attended TTHS in the 50s. After serving a stint in the Navy, Dreesen teamed with Tim Reid of *WKRP of Cincinnati* fame and toured the country as the first and only black and white comedy team. Later, he soloed as a standup comedian and headlined for stars Sammy Davis Jr., Dean Martin, and most notably, Frank Sinatra for fourteen years. He has also appeared on numerous TV talk shows, sitcoms, dramas, and in movies.

Dreesen's fame, especially in the Chicago area, sparked an idea within the TALF Board. They asked him if he would do a benefit show for the public in Thornton High School's auditorium. Dreesen agreed, and TALF's first major fundraising event, *The Tom Dreesen Show and Silent Auction*, was launched in 2006. Over 1,000 people attended. The event grossed over $100,000, but the showstopper was an astonishing announcement from an eccentric alumnus, Fred Furth.

CHAPTER 28

If LaMarr, Chris, Jane, Lorna, Ray, and the other TALF executives thought the gala evening event, *The Tom Dreesen Show and Silent Auction*, had ended with a standing ovation for Tom and a $100,000 gross purse, they were wrong. A tall seventy-two-year-old man wearing a white suit, tinted glasses, and a Panama hat strolled onto the stage with an unlit cigar in one hand and a leash toting his Great Dane, Brandenburg, in the other. He was eccentric West Coast attorney and wine baron Fred Furth—estimated net worth: $311 million.

Fred Furth
Photo courtesy of Drew Altizer Photography

Fred grew up in Harvey and graduated from Thornton in the early 50s. He went on to become one of the most successful trial lawyers in the country. He litigated national antitrust class action suits, but his passion was advocating for the rights of injured citizens and the underprivileged. "I'm a modern-day legal Robin Hood," he told the

Santa Rosa Press Democrat. He had won a $172 million class action suit against Walmart on behalf of its employees who had been denied breaks. Aside from his lucrative West Coast law practice, Fred owned and operated Chalk Hill Winery in the Sonoma Valley where he lived in a complex that included a full equestrian center and a regulation football field.

Onstage, Fred reminisced about growing up in Harvey and benefiting from the great education he attained at Thornton. At the climax of his speech, he announced, "I'll give this school $100,000." Everyone in the auditorium including Brandenburg looked astonished. Earlier, TALF President Jane Martin had declared to the audience TALF's goal of raising $1,000,000 for Thornton's endowment. "When you [TALF] raise $450,000, I'll add $50,000. When you reach $950,000, I'll add the other $50,000."

"After that, people started giving," Ray Jakubiak recalled.

LaMarr, Chris, and Lorna Propes gave over $5,000. Eric Fox, CEO of Irmko Tool and Works and co-founder of Goose Island Brewery, contributed over $10,000, and Jane Martin gave over $25,000.

Dan Ustian, Chair and CEO of Navistar International Corporation contributed more than a generous sum of money; he contributed ideas, support, and his time. Ray Jakubiak worked

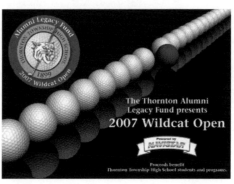

The Thornton Alumni Legacy Fund presents
2007 Wildcat Open

Powered by
NAVISTAR

Proceeds benefit
Thornton Township High School students and programs.

for Dan at Navistar. "Dan got really interested in TALF," Ray said. "He also loved golf. He called me and said, 'Let's have a golf outing and raise money for TALF,' he said, and that became our next TALF event in 2007."

Although golf wasn't LaMarr's favorite sport, he loved the idea and became one of the chief organizers. As a "people person," LaMarr talked both the rich and the not-so-rich into contributing towards, and participating in, the event. It wasn't

Lorna Propes, Jane Martin and Dan Ustian
Photo courtesy of Thornton Alumni Legacy Fund

difficult to talk Tom Dreesen into taking part in the outing. Tom loved Thornton, Harvey, and golf. He and LaMarr forged a friendship that continued throughout LaMarr's life.

LaMarr never forgot the people who positively influenced him, and he used the golf outing to reunite with some of them. Harry Oryhon, his friend from grade school and a TALF executive, remembered, "LaMarr tracked down Mr. Sidmore [his basketball coach at Warren Palm Elementary School] and invited him and Adeline Anderson, a once-young band director at Warren Palm. They were an "item" back then, but the relationship never materialized. Adeline never married, and Mr. S had lost his wife. LaMarr played cupid and the two reconnected and later, after meeting at the golf outing, traveled together to Europe."

The golf outing and dinner afterward at Calumet Country Club located in Homewood, a south Chicago suburb, was an enormous success netting over $100,000.

By making the golf outing an annual event and continuing solicitation of donations, TALF's goal of raising one million dollars for Thornton could be reached within a few years. The goal wasn't just to raise money; it was to spend it to save the school and improve its educational programs, extracurricular activities, and facilities.

TALF's initial contribution was $10,000 to restore a yearbook program, an essential historical commodity common to most high schools, rich or poor. Over the next two years, TALF spent nearly $50,000 for the following: interactive world history maps, video equipment, stereo/CD players, Summer Speech Institute, Special Education field trips, newspapers, computer lab equipment, athletic video equipment, theater lighting, an art gallery, Thornton Gospel Choir travel fees, SophistiCats dance troupe supplies/uniforms, Speech Camp fees/travel, a Student Activities Director, and the cheerleaders' summer camp fees.

LaMarr had found his niche as an activist through TALF. Unlike his position at the EEOC, he was busy making positive changes for an educational institution and underprivileged kids. He also considered himself to be a scholar and had been thinking about continuing to work on his doctorate and expanding his major in history to include English.

Dan Ustian, CEO of Navistar, recognized LaMarr's need to be an activist.

"Dan really liked LaMarr," Ray Jakubiak recalled, "and said to me, 'We need to do something for LaMarr.'"

CHAPTER 29

"We're only graduating about 35,000 technicians, total, in this country a year. That includes auto, collision, and diesel, and only about 10% of those graduates are diesel and truck technicians.

In the truck market, I think it is already too late. We're looking at a significant shortfall," Tony Molla, vice president of communications for the National Institute for Automotive Service Excellence, warned during an interview for *Transport Topics* magazine in 2009.

Dan Ustian was aware of Molla's grim statistics and the stats' negative impact for Navistar, owner of international trucks and diesel engines. But Dan was more than the CEO of Navistar. He loved his alma mater, Thornton High School, supported TALF's mission, and had a deep respect and liking for LaMarr.

Synthesizing the needs of his company, his former high school, TALF, and his friends, Dan partnered with Thornton Township High School District 205 and created *The Academy of Truck & Diesel Technology*—a three-year National Automotive Technicians Education Foundation (NATEF) Certification Program. More importantly, he put LaMarr in charge of it.

With the help of Roger Williams from Navistar, LaMarr formed and propelled *The Academy of Truck & Diesel Technology*,

Dan Ustian and Dr. J. Kamala Buckner launch The Academy of Truck & Diesel Technology and new Tech Building at Thornton Township High School.

Photo courtesy of Thornton Alumni Legacy Fund

a full-time task. Navistar funded approximately one million dollars for twenty-four engines, four trucks, specialized tools, lesson plans, labs, and workstations. Dr. J. Kamala Buckner, Superintendent of High School District 205, agreed to kick in an additional $1.3 million to renovate the Thornton Tech Building if students from the other district high schools, Thornridge and Thornwood, would be allowed to participate in the program. LaMarr, Williams, Navistar, and TALF agreed.

It would take three years for students to complete the program. Each year, forty-eight sophomores from all three district schools with a minimum grade-point-average of 2.5 could enroll in the program. If they successfully completed the program, they would become certified diesel repair and maintenance mechanics and eligible to work on diesel engines and trucks anywhere in the country. District 205, Navistar, and TALF launched *The Academy of Truck & Diesel*

LaMarr at The Academy of Truck & Diesel Technology and new Tech Building launch

Photo courtesy of Thornton Alumni Legacy Fund

Technology at the newly renovated Tech Building at Thornton in August of 2009.

Over the next several years, LaMarr and Chris enjoyed a stable life residing in their Naperville condo. Chris worked full-time as a financial adviser. LaMarr, although still employed with the EEOC, worked diligently to keep the Navistar diesel certification program running. His closest friends had all moved far away, and the diesel program had become his surrogate buddy. HK's successful career in international trading and merchandising had forced him to move to Beijing, China. Victor had established himself as a respected physician in Louisiana, and Harry Oryhon would be leaving his dentistry business in the Chicago area and moving to Franklin, Tennessee.

TALF gave purpose and rejuvenation to LaMarr's and Chris's lives. They worked hard with other TALF executive members to organize the first Thornton Hall of Fame. LaMarr, who had spent hours combing through yearbooks in the Thornton High School library to find alumni to speak to Thornton students, used the same method to identify Hall of Fame nominees. The first Thornton Township Hall of Fame dinner/ceremony took place in May of 2010. TALF inducted eight faculty members and sixty alumni including: Major League Baseball Hall of Famer player/ manager/broadcaster Lou Boudreau (posthumously), comedian/ actor/writer Tom Dreesen, first woman 100-meter Olympic gold medalist Betty Robinson (posthumously), all five members of the R&B/soul/doo-wop group The Dells, Metropolitan Opera singer Wendy White, and TV/stage/screen actors Bill Hayes and Stan DeSantis (posthumously).

One month later, on June 4th, LaMarr and Chris remarried in a civil ceremony in the DuPage County Courthouse. Few people knew they had divorced in 1991, and fewer knew they hadn't been officially married since the divorce. Their reasons for legally remarrying were vague, even to Chris. "I'm not exactly sure why we decided to do it," Chris said. "I know it made doing our taxes easier." One can easily speculate that working together to resurrect their beloved alma mater might have brought them closer together and influenced their decision.

That first Hall of Fame event grossed $73,000, and over the next two years, the golf outings, subsequent Hall of Fame events, and private donations totaled $240,000. TALF awarded Thornton $78,675 for designated programs and facilities.

Perhaps the proudest achievement for TALF and LaMarr came in May of 2012, and it had nothing to do with raising money. Thornton's *Academy of Truck & Diesel Technology* graduated its first class. Thirty-two students had completed the three-year National Automotive Technicians Education Foundation (NATEF) Certification Program and were crowned certified diesel mechanics. Twenty-seven planned to seek advanced engineering degrees, and six landed jobs in the automotive, truck, or diesel engine industries. One hundred and fifty new students had enrolled in the program for the coming year.

"At the graduation ceremony," Ray Jakubiak said. "The parents of these kids were so proud."

It was also a proud day for LaMarr having overseen the program, but he had another unexpected proud day coming. In September of that year, TALF held the Seventh Annual Wildcat Golf Open and Dinner. At the banquet dinner, Tom Dreesen entertained and made a surprise presentation of a TALF Lifetime Achievement Award to LaMarr. Neither LaMarr nor Chris had seen this coming. LaMarr was speechless. After speaking briefly and fielding congratulations from the guests that topped 200, he sat down, exhausted.

LaMarr seemed to be hyperventilating; he was breathless ... something was wrong.

CHAPTER 31

Fall, 2012

"LaMarr was having a hard time breathing, but he put off going to the doctor," Chris recalled. "He slammed open the sliding glass door [in their condo] to get some air. 'We've got to go and see a doctor,' I said."

The doctor at Edwards Hospital in Naperville examined LaMarr and ordered a series of tests. Within a few weeks, LaMarr completed a battery of tests which included blood analysis, a chest x-ray, a CT scan, and later, a biopsy.

The attending physician conferred with LaMarr and Chris about the results. "I wish I had better news. LaMarr, you have a form of thymus cancer. The thymus is a small organ that lies in the upper chest above the heart and under the breastbone. There are two kinds of thymus cancer: thymoma and thymic carcinoma. You have the second type. Unlike thymoma, in thymic carcinoma, the cancer cells do not look like the normal cells of the thymus and grow more quickly and are more likely to spread to other parts of the body. About one in every five thymus cancers is a thymic carcinoma. Thymic carcinoma is more difficult to treat than thymoma, but it can be treated."

After discussing the various treatment options, LaMarr and Chris left the hospital in shock. Neither spoke until they entered their car.

"Are you okay?" LaMarr asked Chris.

Over the next two years, LaMarr endured aggressive cancer treatments.

"They blasted him with radiation and chemotherapy. He was in the hospital for the chemo," Chris said.

All through his treatments, LaMarr did not advertise his illness.

"I remember calling him and leaving a message to call me back," Ray Jakubiak remembered, "but he didn't return my call for a few weeks. When he did call, he apologized and said he had been in the hospital but just said it was something routine, so I didn't press him."

"Looking back, he'd always call me back after I'd try to reach him, but he took longer to call back during that time. When I found out about his cancer much later, it hurt me that he didn't tell me, me being his friend and a doctor, even though there was nothing more I could do," Victor Jackson said.

"He was a strong person," Chris recalled. "He never complained, ever."

All through his therapy, he stayed active with TALF.

In 2013, the organization worked to restore the Lou Boudreau Room at Thornton High School. The room which honored the Major League Baseball Hall of Famer and more Thornton alumni had long been a museum of Thornton history but had been neglected for decades. With TALF's support, Laura and Jerry Kaufman, alumni from the class of 1974, worked hard to renovate and update this historic room. LaMarr participated in the project and spoke at the reopening ceremony on October 26th.

By 2014, TALF had reached a fundraising milestone of $450,000. Fred Furth made good on his promise and added

LaMarr greeting Lou Boudreau Jr. after the ceremony

Photo courtesy of
Thornton Alumni Legacy Fund

another fifty grand, and they were halfway to their one million-dollar goal. Fred celebrated by holding a gala dinner party at his Lake Forest, Illinois estate. LaMarr, Chris, and the other TALF executives attended. LaMarr enjoyed the festivity and appeared to be feeling better. Although the cancer was not in remission, it hadn't progressed aggressively.

TALF announced that LaMarr would be inducted into the Thornton Hall of Fame alongside other inductees in the spring of 2015. The Hall of Fame induction took place at the high school in the afternoon and later that evening at a banquet /induction ceremony. The afternoon session included a tour of the Navistar Diesel Program that LaMarr had helped initiate. In the evening, along with presentations and speeches from Hall of Fame recipients, an alumnus from the Navistar Diesel Program spoke about how the curriculum gave him a second chance in life to make a living and find a place in the world. LaMarr choked up from the speech and held back tears. The printed program featured a photo and written profile of each inductee. A portion of LaMarr's life synopsis read as follows:

> After leaving EEOC, he's worked as an independent contractor/writer/researcher focused on issues of educational achievement of low-income students and students of color. This work reflects his strong commitment to social and community betterment and

to expanded opportunities for all.

LaMarr is a charter member of the (2004) Thornton Alumni Legacy Fund (TALF) that would simply not exist without his efforts. Through his concerted efforts and those of his fellow alumni, a 501c3 was created and launched an endowment called "Vanguard 300," which is now the cornerstone of TALF's fundraising efforts. As TALF gained traction, LaMarr has been involved in and leading every event including Alumni Day, The Distinguished Speakers Program, re-establishment of the Thorntonite Yearbook, the Navistar Diesel Program—all of which have his imprint. He nurtured the relationship between TALF and Dan Ustian '68, former President and CEO of Navistar and sponsor of the Wildcat Golf Outing. Not only did the support of our golf outing help with fundraising, but the Navistar Diesel Engine Program continues to guide students on a productive path. He [LaMarr] was an inspiration for Wildcats for over 50 years, first as a leader during his student years, and most recently as a guiding light for TALF and all who cared about the greatness of TTHS.

"Attending Thornton," LaMarr says, "was, and continues to be, a defining experience in my life." It is precisely because of the profound and enduring impact of his Thornton years, LaMarr says, that he joined in becoming one of the founding members of the Thornton Alumni Legacy Fund. "So well aware of the rich benefits I received from my Thornton education, I wanted to help current students in some measure to have the rewarding 'Thornton Experience' that so many in my generation had." LaMarr says that he will be forever eternally grateful for his Thornton years, because it was "here at Thornton that I met my fellow classmate and the love of my life, my wife of forty years, Chris LaVette."

Nowhere in the synopsis nor at the Hall of Fame events that day was there mention of his cancer, and nothing in LaMarr's demeanor indicated that he was suffering. Afterward, however, he paid a price for his active behavior earlier that day. He grew very tired in the weeks that followed and symptoms of his disease - shortness of breath and fatigue - reemerged.

He and Chris returned to Edwards Hospital. After more tests, the oncologist said, "I can't do anything more for you."

Disheartened but undeterred, Chris later said, "We were not giving up." They sought a second opinion from Dr. Philip Bonomi, a leading oncologist in the Chicago area. Dr. Bonomi was known for treating all kinds of cancer and worked primarily through Rush University Medical Center and Rush Oak Park Hospital. Dr. Bonomi didn't offer false hope. "Thymic carcinoma is more likely to recur than thymoma," he informed them, but he did offer to try experimental treatments and retry treatments LaMarr had previously undergone.

"LaMarr liked him," Chris recalled, and LaMarr's renewed spirit gave him strength to endure more therapy and continue writing and working for TALF. He became less private about his condition and began talking to his closest friends about the cancer.

"He called and told me about the cancer," Dr. Green said. "LaMarr had been working with me for the Cleveland Public schools. It was one of the saddest moments of my life."

HK (Harry Hall) said, "I learned about it [the cancer] secondhand. Our friend, Vic [Jackson] told me."

Over the next few years, LaMarr looked forward to

HK (Harry) Hall, LaMarr, and Victor Jackson
Photo courtesy of Thornton Alumni Legacy Fund

organizing and attending TALF events. On November 2, 2018, his oldest and closest friends, HK and Victor, showed up for

Chris and LaMarr at the Hall of Fame
banquet, November 2, 2018
Photo courtesy of Thornton Alumni Legacy Fund

the Hall of Fame festivities. The reunion rejuvenated LaMarr; he was ecstatic.

As a physician, Victor recognized the effect LaMarr's exuberance that night would have on him. "I knew, because of his condition, he would pay a price for overextending himself."

Victor was right.

LaMarr became very weak during the following days. Knowing he would rally after a few weeks of rest, he accepted the weakness and continued writing and reading; however, this time was different. He didn't recover as quickly or as completely from the weakness as he had before.

After the Christmas/New Year's Day holidays, his condition worsened. Dr. Bonomi, having applied all the treatments available to LaMarr's rare form of cancer, said the words Chris and LaMarr dreaded and had heard years earlier from the oncologist at Edwards Hospital, "I can't do anything more for you."

By late March of 2019, LaMarr could barely leave the condo. The advice given by Dr Bonomi and the attending medical staff was to consider hospice care. When Chris and LaMarr got into their car after hearing this recommendation, LaMarr made the same comment to Chris he had seven years ago when they learned he had cancer.

"Are you okay?" he asked.

CHAPTER 32

"Hospice care is a special kind of care that focuses on the quality of life for people and their caregivers who are experiencing an advanced, life-limiting illness."

That's how The American Cancer Society defines "hospice."

LaMarr embraced "the quality of life for people and their caregivers" part of that definition. The alternative would have been in-hospital care, but that meant being away from Chris and the condo where he felt comfortable with friends and family. "People came to the house while I was at work," Chris said.

When Harry Oryhon received the message that LaMarr was not doing well, he drove up from Tennessee and they reminisced about Warren Palm Elementary School. "LaMarr remarked about how he never felt repressed by the white community back then like blacks in the South were experiencing. 'It was like an island of tranquility,' he said."

"I saw LaMarr maybe three days before he passed," HK said. "Over the past two or three months before he passed, I tried to visit him at least once a week. LaMarr wanted to see everyone before he died, but during the last days he didn't necessarily want them to see him. As usual, he was more concerned about their feelings than his own. I asked, 'Do you remember certain football plays over all the others?' LaMarr said that he did and started describing [not his own performance] a great block some guy made for him."

Victor came with the intention of rallying his best friend and encouraging him to take a walk with him to renew his strength. "When I saw his weak condition, I knew that would not be a good idea."

Jack Browers, LaMarr and Chris's brother-in-law, his wife (Chris's older sister) and their children visited LaMarr during this time. "We saw him a couple of weeks before he died," Jack recalled. "We were getting ready to leave, and he was really weak. He said, 'No, don't leave because this is something we always did in church.' We grabbed hands, and we sang, 'God be with you. God be with you. God be with you until we meet again.'"

In his last few days, LaMarr took the initiative to call people he hadn't seen to say good-bye. He called Dr. Green (of course) and Tom Dreesen.

"Nine days before he died, he called and suggested my [latest] book be a part of the MSU curriculum," said Dr. Green.

Tom recalled, "He called me a few days before he passed and told me he only had days left and how glad he was that we were friends and how much that meant to him. It was heart-wrenching for me, but I hung on to my composure because he was hanging on to his. We talked at great length about many things but most of all our love of Harvey, TTHS and the children attending and living in the community."

LaMarr Thomas died at 5:36 p.m., April 25, 2019.

CHAPTER 33

June 8, 2019

It was a near-perfect afternoon—70 degrees, a little cloudy, but with neither rain nor heavy winds predicted. It would have been a perfect day for athlete LaMarr Thomas to carry, catch, or throw a football across the gridiron, or scholar LaMarr to sit outside on his patio and read history books, or activist LaMarr to lead discussions about world problems and solutions with other activists on a college campus.

LaMarr's family picked this perfect day to celebrate his life at St. Andrew United Methodist Church in Homewood, Illinois. Relatives, friends, acquaintances, former teammates, classmates, and colleagues packed into the lobby. As more people arrived, the chatter and laughter grew louder and reverberated throughout the church. The mood sobered as the small groups dispersed and entered the church sanctuary. The filled pews forced late-comers to stand in the back.

Ray Jakubiak addressed the congregation from the podium. He

Ray Jakubiak
Photo courtesy of
Blink of an Eye Productions

welcomed them on behalf of Chris, Tina, and himself. "The overflow of support [for Chris and Tina] just shows you what kind of guy LaMarr was. He was so appreciated, loved, and adored, and why? Because he treated people so kindly. . . When he talked to you, you felt you that you were the world's most important person. LaMarr would never let me say this publicly, but a lot of TALF'S success was due to *his* hard work, *his* drive, and *his* association with the organization. . . He was a gentle, and yet fierce soul."

Linnetta Taylor
Photo courtesy of
Blink of an Eye Productions

Ray introduced Linnetta Taylor, LaMarr's friend since his childhood when they both sang in their church choir. She sang "What I Did for Love." Her performance provoked applause and tears.

Dr. Green delivered the eulogy. He started by saying that he had met LaMarr through MSU Head Football Coach Duffy Daugherty in the fall of 1966. "LaMarr was different from the

Dr. Robert L. Green
Photo courtesy of
Blink of an Eye Productions

other ballplayers. He could think. He could write, and he was a scholar who was concerned about social injustice. We wrote together. We published together. We put together (and he did most of the writing) a major article on historic black colleges and why these colleges should survive. I met with all the presidents of the historic black colleges. They took his rationale [the article] to the White House to be used at the federal level for funding. LaMarr could sit with the most radical students and talk sense. One day, Bob Little (Malcom X's brother) and about eight or nine angry black students came to see me. They wanted an all-black college at Michigan State (something I didn't believe in). LaMarr stood up and said, 'I'm going to tell all of you something. Those of you who want an all-black school, you can get it.' And he named about nine different schools. 'But we're here, and let's stay here and make this a better place,' and that made sense to them."

Victor Jackson came from Louisiana to speak. He talked about how he, HK, and LaMarr grew up together in Markham and created a fierce competitive mentality playing baseball and basketball with and against each other. "And LaMarr could sing. He joined the church choir, and when he sang, he could

Dr. Victor Jackson
Photo courtesy of
Blink of an Eye Productions

make it rain! Because of LaMarr's singing, I and other people joined the church. He took that singing to the basketball team." Victor reminisced about the coach getting mad when they sang on the bus after a loss. He recalled the time they roomed together in Nashville when Victor went to medical school, and LaMarr attracted students from nearby universities to come to their apartment to discuss social issues. "Those students were mesmerized by him."

Carl Barnhill
Photo courtesy of
Blink of an Eye Productions

Carl Barnhill, a football teammate at Thornton, spoke next. "There isn't a person here today whose life hasn't been enriched by LaMarr," he began his speech. "LaMarr had all the rare qualities of a great human being. If he wanted to be a politician, he would have been the best politician this world has ever seen. He would have been able to draw people across the aisle and do what's right. If he wanted to be a CEO of a company, he would have been the best businessman for that company. He could be anyone he wanted to be, and he was exactly what he wanted to be."

HK (Harry) Hall
Photo courtesy of
Blink of an Eye Productions

Ray opened the floor for comments.

HK (Harry) Hall shared his first encounter with LaMarr when they were on the same Little League team. "He said to me 'I believe in team' at only eight or nine years old."

Linnetta Taylor who met LaMarr in the church choir felt "honored that he would choose me as a friend." When she visited him during his final days, LaMarr spoke of how much his sister Tina and his wife Chris meant to him.

Harry Oryhon, his friend from elementary school and high school recalled LaMarr's Elvis impersonation at a school talent show. "We had a friendship that would never die."

Over twenty more people shared

Harry Oryhon
Photo courtesy of
Blink of an Eye Productions

their thoughts, stories, and experiences concerning LaMarr before his brother-in-law, Jack Browers, delivered a closing prayer. Everyone left the same way they had entered—chatting, laughing, and reminiscing. If anyone came to this memorial to mourn LaMarr's death, they may have left disappointed.

This was a celebration of his life.

And God, what a life!

EPILOGUE

Friday, May 8, 2015

LaMarr spoke first. His Hall of Fame acceptance speech mesmerized the audience. Over the years, he had become a dynamic speaker. His speech emphasized attaining human rights, setting goals, tackling adversity, and modeling for youth.

After being introduced, I glanced at my long-time friend, Mark Garry. His expression said, "I don't envy you following that moving oration."

At the lectern, I put my notes aside and spoke impromptu.

"LaMarr just spoke about role models. When I was a freshman at Thornton, LaMarr was a senior. I was the lucky one. Could any freshman have had a better role model than the one I had, senior LaMarr Thomas?"

My rhetorical question evoked a standing ovation. It didn't matter how good or badly I spoke after that. The crowd was on my side because I sided with LaMarr.

I would see LaMarr only one more time after that. We both attended the banquet honoring the next Hall of Fame inductees. Before dinner, LaMarr approached our table and looked directly at me. He greeted and spoke collectively to all ten people seated, but we locked eye contact the whole time. I knew he remembered me and my tribute to him the previous year.

As an adult, he had fought for the disadvantaged with the same passion and determination that he had brandished on the football field. It finally took cancer to take him out, and even that had a rough time.

Tom Dreesen said it best:

"I thought he was one of the finest individuals I've ever met. I know that he is in heaven because if LaMarr Thomas is not in heaven, then there is no heaven. He was a quiet, strong, loving,

---

caring man who will be missed by all who loved him, and that is a lot of folks because all who met him soon loved him."

Photo courtesy of Blink of an Eye Productions

AUTHOR'S FINAL NOTE

August 10, 2021

"Why are you writing this?" Tina Thomas, LaMarr's sole surviving sibling, asked me during our first interview session.

It's not only a fair question but also a common one asked of authors. Sometimes the question is specific to a particular work, and sometimes it's a more general query, "What inspires you to write?" Either way, I always find it difficult to answer.

Some of my more honest author/colleagues will say, "I'm doing it for the money" or "I'm hoping it will make me rich and famous." In my case, it's not for the money. I'm not rich, but I enjoy a generous Illinois Teachers' Retirement pension. All my residuals for this book will go to Thornton Township High School through the Thornton Alumni Legacy Fund.

It's certainly not for fame. My father once told me, "If you're not famous by the time you're sixty-five, you probably won't be, and if you do become famous after sixty-five, it'll probably be for something you don't want to be known for."

Richard Sand, a fellow author/mentor/colleague/friend offered the best answer. I asked him, "Why, as an award-winning author, professor, attorney, and martial arts expert, do you take time to mentor me?"

"Because writing for you, like for me, is a calling," he answered.

As vague as that answer might be, I've stopped exploring its meaning. Few, if any, of my colleagues, friends, or relatives would describe me as religious or spiritual. At the same time, I accept that metaphysical reason for writing about LaMarr.

It is a "calling."

Whether it's from heaven, God, LaMarr, or my own subconscious, I had to author this book, and I'm glad I did. I never really knew LaMarr when he was alive. Having studied him as he studied the world around him, I think I know him now. I know how he lived, and I know why he lived. Moreover, he taught me the right way we should live.